Conflict Imagery

developing a reflective framework

Conflict Imagery

developing a reflective framework

KILEY FLEMING, EdD

www.BookpressPublishing.com

Published in Des Moines, Iowa, by:

Bookpress Publishing
P.O. Box 71532
Des Moines, IA 50325
www.BookpressPublishing.com

Publisher's Cataloging-in-Publication Data

Names: Fleming, Kiley, author.
Title: Conflict Imagery : developing a reflective framework / Kiley Fleming, EdD.
Description: Includes bibliographical references. | Des Moines, IA: Bookpress Publishing, 2023.
Identifiers: LCCN: 2022910932 | ISBN: 978-1-947305-47-2
Subjects: LCSH Interpersonal conflict. | Conflict management. | Conflict (Psychology) |
BISAC BUSINESS & ECONOMICS / Human Resources & Personnel Management |
SELF-HELP / Communication & Social Skills
Classification: LCC HD42 .F54 2023 | DDC 658.45--dc23

First Edition
Printed in the United States of America
10 9 8 7 6 5 4 3 2 1

This book is dedicated to my greatest treasures:
Jamin Matthew, Keziah Elizabeth, and Zebulun David.
Your presence awakened parts of my soul that didn't exist until you
came into the world. Although it may seem strange to dedicate a
book about conflict to your children, in fact the beauty of your lives
is what taught me the power of resiliency and tenacity, without which
the research of this book could not have happened. Thank you for
the overflowing grace and love you bestow upon me. As you each
grow into your own unique capacity, it is my fervent hope that you
rest assuredly in your chosen identities.

CONTENTS

ACKNOWLEDGMENTS

I would like to thank everyone who meaningfully walked alongside me as I learned, often through trial and error, how to become a better manager of conflict.

To the principals at Bookpress Publishing for championing this project and believing it could be brought to fruition in a way that carried my voice and intention.

To my team at Iowa Mediation Service, for cheering me on and continually demonstrating the "onward and upward" spirit. You motivated me beyond words to pursue the heart of this book.

To Jen Tischler, for graciously providing your creative gifts by developing the graphics in this book. You somehow captured the elements of my mind and manifested them onto paper.

To Kathy Eckert, for introducing me to the artful and intuitive practice of conflict management. A better mentor, collaborator, and true friend I won't find again in this lifetime.

To the research subjects, although I cannot reveal your names, I am indebted by your willingness to participate in my study. Your insights and wisdom are what propelled this book.

To Creighton University, for providing the foundation that challenged me to grow.

Most importantly, a deep and abiding heart of gratitude to all who explore the imagery found within. You ignite my spirit, curiosity, and purpose.

Introduction

When an elephant is in the room, there are many ways to address it. You could ignore it, but it might wreck your furniture. You could run from it, but it would likely catch up. You could yell at it, make it stampede, but that might make matters worse. Or you could decide to name it for what it is: a large, gray mammal with thick skin—a pachyderm. To describe the elephant as a tiny, feather-like bird would be laughably disingenuous, and furthermore, there's no reason to describe the elephant as anything other than what it actually is: an incredible creature with fascinating characteristics. It's the largest land animal, in fact, and the lion is her only natural predator.

Some might feel there is an elephant in the room surrounding the concept of this book, *Conflict Imagery: Developing a Reflective Framework*. Surely an author who has weathered a difficult divorce could be no card-carrying expert on successful conflict resolution. Clearly she was unable to deal with the conflict in her marriage and is therefore in no position to discuss the throes of conflict and how to navigate it. That's the elephant in the room. Conflict resolution is the elephant and divorce is the lion preying upon it. The two happened to meet in the desert of life, and one temporarily prevailed. *Temporarily* is the operative word here because the elephant didn't die in the battle. In fact, now she's stronger from the scars. The marks are simple reminders from this time period that tell the story of what was gained and lost as a result of the journey. The best gifts from this season of my life were the realizations that people have a deep capacity for growth, that meaningful change and learning can occur in any situation, and that resilience is a huge part of the human condition.

Navigating through a divorce also revealed that the perspective of conflict resolution isn't the healthiest mindset for most people. The concept of resolution assumes a position of win or lose and measures success upon a final, permanent outcome. Instead, I now embrace the framework of conflict *management* after coming out the other side of the separation. In fact, divorce is a great metaphor for conflict management because even after the judge signs the decree, it is rarely just "over." Most people spend years dealing with the relationships of all parties involved, so it requires a continual re-evaluation of needs, positions, and values. It requires a management mindset.

Instead of thinking about this divorced author as a failure at conflict *resolution* (which perhaps she is), think about her as a champion for hope-filled conflict *management*. After all, she may find herself in the desert again sometime and see a lion coming her way, but the scars are evidence of stronger survival skills. The lion may be the king of the jungle, but this elephant is the queen of the desert.

What's Your Wheelhouse?

One hundred and sixty-eight illuminated chairs. This is how many stand on the manicured lawn of the Oklahoma City National Memorial. In 1995, the unimaginable happened when the lives of 168 people ended with terrorist violence.[1] Compared to other tragedies throughout history, 168 lives might sound like a small number until you walk through the memorial. Seeing 168 chairs lined up in nine rows representing the nine floors of the decimated building took my breath away. Then I saw the nineteen tiny chairs for the nineteen tiny souls that were taken from this world far too soon. I didn't live in Oklahoma during this event, nor did I personally know anyone who perished, but I wept at the sight of the little chairs representing the children who died. While I was only in my early twenties when I visited the memorial, the experience is still etched in my mind and scored on my heart—168 chairs.

Why do students visit museums and adults collect antiques? Why do cities invest in historic preservation and archeologists dig to unearth artifacts? Why do lighthouses, shipwrecks, and ancient ruins spark curiosity among tourists? All these efforts and interests represent an innate human desire to create connections.[2] Physical objects are a key method we've learned to use to outwardly demonstrate internal environments, conditions, and values. This has been done since the beginning of time, evident, for example, in the traditions of Egyptians honoring their buried dead with cherished objects now considered obsolete in this modern era. During burial ceremonies, these items were deemed critical for underworld survival. Egyptians believed success hinged upon using these objects in the afterlife.[3] While many of these items—alabaster bottles filled with oils, scarab beetles for protection, canopic jars filled with organs, and death masks—would never be used in funeral proceedings today, we still consider these items a critical testament to the history of a mysterious civilization, and they still carry a strong magical allure.

Similarly, today we see efforts to preserve buildings of historical value, projects far more expensive than simply demolishing and reconstructing. They are often preserved even when the materials and tools used to build them are obsolete in modern architecture. Why go to such lengths to hold onto the material past? Is a vintage postage stamp worth preserving if it can no longer be used to send mail? Is an old coin valuable even if it can't buy anything at the store? Collectors spend many hours and dollars investing in unusable items that tell stories of years gone by. The 168 chairs at the Oklahoma City National Memorial aren't functional because no one is allowed to actually sit on them. This isn't the point. The visionaries of the memorial site understood that a tangible representation of the horrific events of that date could teach more on the topic than any lecture. The chairs serve as an external manifestation of an internal value: the hope that history won't repeat itself if we keep meaningfully sharing lessons about destructive acts.[4]

We can discuss the Mayan ruins and look at pictures, but it's not the same as actually experiencing the tangible setting. That is why people travel for miles to experience it first-hand. We can read about the mystique of Machu Picchu in *National Geographic*, but I'd much rather navigate it myself than rely on the perspectives of others. We can listen to the preacher discuss Babylon from the pulpit or physically walk the ancient streets to get a fuller sense of its history. Recently, I was talking with a colleague about his desire to restore an old municipal golf course in his community back to its original state. We started to discuss his reasons and examine his arguments as a renovation of this magnitude would require substantial resources from City Hall. This friend is a Millennial, and he spoke of his desire to garner his generation's appreciation for the golf course as a piece of history. It's more than 120 years old, the oldest municipal golf course west of the Mississippi. He believed that restoring the golf course to its original design would help the next generation of golfers treasure its historic value in an urban, modern setting. His father was also part of the conversation and posed this challenge to his son:

"City officials are going to want to know what problem this type of renovation is addressing and why taxpayers should care about this project," he said. "Let's think about the Roman Colosseum. Today it is essentially a heap of rocks, but people still visit it in huge numbers. Why? When you can sort through this, then you will know how to present your golf renovation project."

That's when it struck me: tangible objects create imagery for the past. There is an innate desire in all cultures to connect external artifacts to internal values, beliefs, and philosophies.[5] We inform others about our principles through easily understood concrete associations.

Let's break down the concept of why concrete associations must be understood by the audience to have value. Because almost every culture has some form of religious framework, consider a faith-based model. Most people I know understand the Star of David represents Judaism, the cross signifies Christianity, and the star and crescent symbolizes Islam.[6] However, many of my acquaintances would be unable to describe the symbol associated with Taoism. Yet, if I asked them to draw the yin and yang symbol, they could recall it in a heartbeat. Furthermore, most people understand that it represents balance and interconnectedness. Spoiler alert: the yin and yang sign also represents Taoism, a religion rooted in Chinese philosophy and the value of harmony. We see the yin and yang icon everywhere in modern design, and we understand its relevance, but the average Midwestern American raised in a Judeo-Christian setting has no point of reference by which to associate it with Taoism. If I wanted to call to mind a symbol that expresses harmony for this population, would it be better to describe this symbol as yin and yang or the symbol of Taoism? Both use the same black and white circular picture, but fewer Americans can mentally retrieve that symbol as it relates to Taoism. Conversely, I would venture a guess that most Taiwanese would have no trouble mentally picturing the symbol for Taoism, a major religion of Taiwan.

Context matters. Associations matter. The ease with which a person can retrieve a mental model matters. The human brain will seek the shortest distance between two points, so it is critical to ask the brain to draw upon what it has readily available.

Yin and Yang Symbol **vs.** Taoism Symbol

This is both the yin and yang symbol and the symbol for Taoism.

Even though we logically understand that to have the most power the examples we use in real life need to resonate with our audience, we still tend to provide illustrations from our own point of view, our own wheelhouse. Ironically, before writing this book, I'd been using "wheelhouse" frequently without knowing its origin or full meaning for sure, so I decided to research the phrase. I didn't have to spend much time on the internet to learn that a wheelhouse is the command center for the captain of a ship.[7] Who knew? My guess is probably lots of people wiser than me, nautical and not, and now this term is officially in my wheelhouse. (See what I did there?) All kidding aside, it is a good reminder that the cues we provide to others carry more power when they resonate with *them*. Our own comfort, however, rests in our individual framework developed over time and through experience, and this framework is what we tend to draw upon when we communicate, especially when we communicate about something abstract, internal, or invisible.

During a recent communication training I conducted with a team of attorneys, a participant used "Easy Like Sunday Morning" by Lionel Richie to characterize someone, and I understood what she was trying to communicate—the person she was describing was laid back. Thinking the reference was clear enough, I began to move on through the training materials, but another participant asked us to pause for a moment. She was confused by the message because she didn't know the song. Oops. Perhaps I should have gathered feedback from the group to ensure we were all on the same page. After all, this was a workshop about the development of communication skills. It hadn't dawned on me that some might be unfamiliar with the reference. Didn't everyone know the master of swoon and swagger, Mr. Lionel Richie? I guess we hadn't all jammed to "Dancing on the Ceiling" as children while we were grounded in our bedrooms. Clearly, lyrics can't convey meaning if others in the group don't know them.

My sincerest apologies to you, Lionel, on behalf of everyone missing out on your talents. You're still one of my favorites and thank you for getting me through many a hard time as an adolescent.

Another example of unintentional miscommunication happens often in teleconferencing: People from various time zones schedule a meeting indicating a clear start time without clarifying the appropriate time zone. I was an offender myself recently when I scheduled a meeting for a group where all US time zones (even Hawaii) were represented. I indicated the meeting would start at 1 p.m. Someone jokingly replied, "Is this 1 p.m. Eastern Standard Time or 1 p.m. Kiley Time?" Guilty as charged. There I was, teaching that words have meaning and that we need to be careful so our perspective tries to include others, yet even a simple meeting notice can reveal how often we rest on our own worldview. Inside my busy little mind, I had these colleagues working from the same clock as me. If only they could have seen the invisible timepiece in my brain. Why yes, the meeting is at 1 p.m. Kiley Time. Better yet, the meeting is at 1 p.m. Central Standard Time. Even better, the meeting is at 11 a.m. PST, 1 p.m. CST, and 2 p.m. EST to cover the broadest time zones of the group.

Have you ever had an ache or pain inside your body that you wanted someone else to understand, often your doctor, but you couldn't exactly put it into words? This is another everyday example of the difficulty of connecting the unseen abstract with the tangible concrete. Since I'm no medical doctor, the proper use of medical terminology to describe my internal state isn't my bailiwick, so my common coping strategy is to provide terms I *am* comfortable with to better connect with my doctor. For example, I had an unexpected need for a pacemaker to be put in during my late thirties. As such, I wasn't the typical, older cardiac patient this doctor would see. My pacemaker was set within the normal range for its usual patients (presumably much older than me), and I had a difficult time adjusting to the new device trying to regulate my heart rate. The cardiologist was trying to figure out my symptoms, and I struggled for the right words. Then, it hit me. The sensation was like the feeling people often get before they have to go on a big stage, perform in an important recital, or give a speech to a large audience. He instantly understood, and his face lit up when I described this to him. That constant feeling of being in a physical state similar to being hyper-nervous was something he could associate with. We were then able to discuss a new, lower setting for my device. I had made a meaningful connection for him regarding the abstract aspect of the situation—my subjective experience with the medical device implanted in my body—by describing an external situation most people can relate to—performance jitters.

Whenever we try to describe emotions, symptoms, or personal perspective, we often turn to the concrete—architecture, religion, sports, medicine, et cetera—in the hopes that our audience can associate external topics with our internal experience. Why couldn't we do the same with conflict and how best to manage it? Like my pacemaker symptoms, just because something isn't seen doesn't mean it isn't real. In fact, many of the most impactful things in this world can't be touched, seen, or heard. Since the beginning of time, wars have been fought over ideas of faith, the treatment of others, and safety. Wars over literal boundary lines or monetary settlements are much easier to contextualize and therefore remedy faster than wars about steadfast beliefs or cultural traditions. Just because you can't create a fence around my religious views or put a price on my faith doesn't make it any less powerful to me. The fence-line of my devotions is deeply rooted within me and are ingrained in my identity and how I define myself. I'm not likely to be easily convinced to draw new boundary lines around my faith to appease someone else's desire to remap my beliefs. This is one example of why we have witnessed wars continuing through the ages. Study the history of Israel if you aren't so sure.[8] Further, there are a myriad of other reasons why conflict pervades the world. Most trial attorneys will tell you that transactional disputes are much easier to frame for a judge or jury than matters of the heart, where the context can vary widely from person to person.[9]

If conflict is so enduring, how do we change the conversation to create roadmaps for meaningful navigation? Imagery. Imagination. Images. These are powerful keys to building awareness, empathy, understanding, and identification with the unseen—bridging the gap between the abstract and the concrete to create meaning. When we have collectively defined meaning, we have opportunities for dialogue. When we have dialogue, we have opportunities for understanding. And when we have understanding, we have opportunities for change. True, enduring change.

Imagery Touchpoints:

1. What are some objects, collections, tourist sites, or symbols you are drawn to? Ponder why these have personal meaning to you. Is there something or someone from your past who informed your impression of these areas of your life?

2. Do you have emotional ties, positive or negative, with certain scents? Places? Activities? Dig a bit deeper and try to visualize a journalist watching you experience these things. What would they photograph? What would they write about? What would the headline be? In what section of the newspaper would they place the article?

3. If you have a tattoo, what is the image? What makes it significant enough to have it permanently inked on your body? If you don't, what tattoo would you get, and why?

Imagery Snapshot: *The concrete world helps create bridges to the abstract. We bring light to the unseen when we connect it with something tangible. Further, the more universal that concrete tangible is for others, the greater the possibility for enriched meaning to ensue.*

Meet the Players

I would love to say I was the brainchild behind the concepts of imagination and conflict. But because plagiarizing is frowned upon in the written world, I must admit that wiser souls before me have already stamped their impressions about each into history. Here are some of my favorite perspectives.[10]

On imagination:

- "The true sign of intelligence is not knowledge but imagination. For knowledge is limited to all we know now and understand, while imagination embraces the entire world, and all there ever will be to know and understand." [Albert Einstein]

- "Everything you can imagine is real." [Pablo Picasso]

- "You can't depend on your eyes when your imagination is out of focus." [Mark Twain]

- "Imagination does not become great until human beings, given the courage and the strength, use it to create." [Maria Montessori]

- "The world of reality has its limits; the world of imagination is boundless." [Jean-Jacques Rousseau]

- "For me, reason is the natural organ of truth; but imagination is the organ of meaning. Imagination, creating new metaphors or reviving old, is not the cause of truth, but its condition." [C.S. Lewis]

On conflict:

- "Peace is not the absence of conflict; it is the ability to handle conflict by peaceful means." [Ronald Reagan]

- "Difficulties are meant to rouse, not discourage. The human spirit is to grow strong by conflict." [William Ellery Channing]

- "God's love is too great to be confined to any one side of conflict or to any one religion." [Desmond Tutu]

- "The greatest conflicts are not between two people but between one person and himself." [Garth Brooks]

- "We have to adopt a wider perspective, and always find common things between the people of north, east, south, and west. Conflict comes from the basis of differences." [Dalai Lama]

- "In the big factory of perfecting human souls, the Earth was a kind of tumbler. The same as the kind people use to polish rocks. All souls come here to rub the sharp edges off each other. All of us we're meant to be worn smooth by conflict and pain of every kind. To be polished. There was nothing bad about this.

This wasn't suffering, it was erosion. It was just another, a basic, an important step in the refining process." [Chuck Palahniuk]

This book isn't an attempt at redefining conflict or imagination. Its goal, rather, is to help bridge the two concepts to reveal how the process of utilizing our imagination makes clear our guiding principles on conflict. When we identify the unique imagery and illustrations that inform our beliefs about conflict, we become more aware of the ways in which we deal with it. This understanding can steer our approach to conflict management, thereby allowing ourselves to become instruments for the creation of positive outcomes within ourselves and throughout the world. Whether you are involved directly in a conflict situation or engaged in self-conflict, or if your goal is to become an adept practitioner of conflict management, this book is for you. We will learn from each other. Together, we will strive to awaken our inner voice and form our conclusions about conflict through the power of imagination.

The Vocabulary

Let's be intentional. Words are powerful tools. They help chisel and clarify the world. Nowhere is this more relevant, perhaps, than in situations dealing with conflict. Like the old adage, "you are what you eat," you are what you say. Words produce life and function and should therefore require accountability in their use. As such, in this book, I use specific terminology to give us a better vocabulary about conflict and imagination, but you may end up using your own set of terms and definitions to explain your perspectives on the topic, and that's entirely fine. In fact, I wholly support this pursuit and encourage and challenge you to think about the language you use. The opportunity for lyricism rises every time we communicate with others, so think about how you use words to create the message you intend. For me, I am most comfortable with the following terms:

Conflict Management vs Conflict Resolution

The term "conflict resolution" implies that every conflict must end with absolute agreement or complete peace to be considered successful.[11] This sends the message that conflict is inherently negative and should be avoided. Assuming something needs to be resolved suggests it would be better gone. However, history has continually demonstrated that challenges, conflicts, and complications provide rich opportunities for some of the most creative and resourceful results to spring forth. "Conflict management" captures this nuance by suggesting that conflict is a natural part of life that can be managed in effective and constructive ways that foster learning, growth, and development.

Practitioner vs Expert

From my background, managing conflict is based on the notion that it is a reciprocal process. Everyone involved has not only the opportunity, but the responsibility to educate, empower, and engage each other in that process. No one is a better expert on your feelings and position in a conflict than yourself. Those who are part of the dispute often know it better than anyone else ever could. As such, it's more accurate in my opinion to name those helping to address the situation as "practitioner" rather than "expert." A practitioner is a skilled individual who augments themselves with a variety of tools to navigate the environment in which they are serving, and they understand that their role is to help involve and guide people through it in a meaningful way.

Parties vs Clients

Because our goal is conflict management, it is more appropriate to discuss those involved in a conflict as "parties" rather than "clients." Parties are comprised of the individuals active in managing outcomes, whereas clients tend to be those in passive roles usually tied to a legal proceeding. There are times when legal platforms are beneficial, but for matters related to this book and for those wishing to engage in empowered conflict management, it's more constructive to consider people as parties within a dispute rather than clients outside of it. This gives them the necessary permission to be the experts of their situations.

Imagination vs Pretending

At times, the concept of "imagination" is confused with "pretending," because we encourage children to use their imaginations when teaching them new concepts. As a result, in adulthood, we often associate using our imaginations with childlike behavior. Pretending is part of a make-believe process where we are given permission to dabble with constructs in whatever way we wish. Imagination, however, is the intentional use of mental pictures and images to illuminate and illustrate an internal state.

After reviewing this list, if you choose to use a different set of terms, go for it. I simply ask that you deliberately evaluate the language you decide to use. As you read this book, it may be helpful to seek other resources from authorities in fields you respect to see how they use language. You have my permission to eavesdrop on conversations among people you wish to emulate. Pick up a newspaper. Read a good book or blog. Watch a compelling movie. Listen to an inspiring song. Observe a powerful roadside billboard. How do they use their words to create their intended effect? Then, decide how you want to be a craftsman of your language. Use your imagination to create your vocabulary.

Because conversations about conflict can be weighty, this book will respectfully discuss the concepts of conflict and imagery while infusing levity and personal experience with professional research along the way. Many experts have already provided scholarly rigor on the topic, so this book was designed using a more playful—yet still highly practical—framework. Language is important, but reverence for it doesn't mean these lessons must be stifling or formal to be informative, meaningful, and impactful. There is no more critical a situation in which to use creative, lighthearted communication than in the management of conflict.

Imagery Touchpoints:

1. How do you feel about the definitions provided? Do they convey the meaning you would like to instill as you move forward with conflict management efforts? What other words might you use instead?

2. Think about a situation in which an incorrect word was inadvertently used. What did it do in that situation? Did it create laughter, insight anger, or cause confusion? How did the experience of using this word change the intended outcome?

3. Consider a situation in which you saw someone navigate conflict well. Write the adjectives you would use to describe that person and the people involved in the situation. Use descriptive words to create a mental picture of the situation prior to their intervention and then another mental picture of the state afterward. Be as expressive as possible.

Imagery Snapshot: *The words we use matter. Even when we have the best intentions, let's not rest on our laurels regarding our language simply because we desire to bring good things with what we say. Every time we speak, impact needs to dovetail with intent.*

Becoming Pro-Conflict—
a Professional in Conflict, That Is...

After more than twenty years of navigating professional fields and parenting adventures that involved various aspects of conflict, when I embarked upon my journey through my doctoral dissertation, it seemed only natural that it would parlay with my inquiry about conflict management. Specifically, I wanted to learn more about the magic of mediation. Having worked in human resources and organizational development consulting before starting a career as the Executive Director for a non-profit mediation company in Iowa, it was fitting to study alternative dispute resolution. Although I had a plethora of experiences related to conflict management, both personally and professionally, it wasn't until I embarked upon my career as a professional mediator that I started to truly see and understand the wonder of mediation.

As a mother of three kids and a human resources practitioner for years, I went to my first mediation with an abundance of confidence. A seasoned mediator and colleague, Kathy, was invited to observe and provide mentorship after the first mediation session. It quickly became apparent that simply knowing all the rote steps involved in the mediation process doesn't necessarily lend itself to successful outcomes. Kathy patiently, graciously, and delicately walked me through our mediation strategy to point out areas of success and shortfall. In hindsight, Kathy was generous with the successes she found in my "performance" as they were *far* outweighed by the shortcomings that day. We laugh about it now and love to use it as an example in our Introduction to Mediation Training that we conduct for new mediators in our state. Using the word "rebuttal" to ask for a simple response didn't make for my finest mediation debut. (Thank you, Kathy, for sticking by my side. You likely wondered why the organization hired me to be the Executive Director when I was so green when it came to mediation skills. I'm indebted to you for skillfully unearthing potential in me!)

Besides being a rather humbling experience, that first day of mediation revealed that successful mediations are truly about nuance, intuition, and flexibility. Since that time years ago, I have witnessed people go through our training and show remarkable mediation skills. I've also seen other people receive the same training and never quite implement the fine touch required to elicit the best possible outcomes for parties in dispute. I am now more confident than ever that a person doesn't need a PhD, EdD, JD, PsyD, MS, BA, or any other academic or professional designation to navigate conflict in a meaningful and productive way. In fact, in many cases, this alphabet soup behind a person's name can actually act as a hindrance to successfully navigating conflict. Instead, those who can tap into their instincts are the ones who best swim the waters of conflict management. And yet, because training and education are wonderful ways to elicit the fullest potential from learners, I knew that somehow there had to be a way to train practitioners of conflict management that tapped into their own unique instincts. Furthermore, the platform needed to be more universal—not just for mediators, but for *anyone* interested in skillfully managing conflict.

While pondering the challenges behind conflict management training, I decided to take a broader view about training in general. When some people facilitate, coach, or train, it fails to make an enduring impression. Yet others make a lasting mark. Why is this? Considering my own personal experiences and observations, it seems to come down to the approach utilized by the trainer. I've seen people attempt to teach others by trying to convince the audience to embrace the trainer's personal values, beliefs, philosophies, and constitutions. This method often falls short because it's based on the trainer's vantage point and not the learner's. Remember, we are naturally designed and more comfortable leaning upon our own background when attempting to connect with others, so it makes sense that this model of training is frequently used because we tend to teach what we're familiar with. Because of this phenomenon, I knew I would need to be careful when studying the topic of mediation and conflict management to ensure I wasn't inadvertently looking for things that confirmed my own views, biases, or perspectives. It's normal to seek what is self-validating, so it was important to find a way to study mediation without projecting my personal belief that good mediators are amazing transformers of conflict. Hence, I needed to decide on an approach that would insulate me from myself. I had hoped that the eventual outcome from the research would be training material, a curriculum, or a book like the one you are currently holding that would keep the end-user—*you*—in mind.

Having learned a lesson from my first mediation disaster, I was admittedly somewhat naïve coming into the research aspect of my dissertation.[12] I knew I didn't want the research on conflict to revolve around just statistics or quantifiable data. These are important, no doubt about it, but I felt like the missing pieces were these practitioners' own understanding and stories. Enough literature and information about the nuts and bolts of mediation already exist. The mediation process is well-documented. Instead, my goal was to elevate what was already understood and use the wisdom and insights of skilled mediators to paint a fuller picture about *why* the process works. By telling these stories and painting a more holistic picture of mediation, the research would transcend the field of alternative dispute resolution and apply to anyone interested in the pursuit of successful conflict management. Managers, professionals, parents, coaches, pastors, friends, and anyone involved in interpersonal relationships can benefit from a better understanding of the nature of conflict and a comprehensive toolbox to address it.

With these factors in mind, I used a research approach called transcendental phenomenology. I won't belabor you with details, but this is essentially a philosophy steeped in qualitative practices where the researcher attempts to remove herself from the research outcome so that the voices of the participants really come through. As a reminder, I was already aware of the natural human tendency to draw from our own personal preferences, past experiences, and areas of comfort, so intentionally insulating myself from the research outcomes was important. As an experienced mediator, I decided to use my background in neutrality to craft research questions that were open-ended in nature and not leading to a particular answer. To boil it all down, the research framework was to explore how experienced practitioners of certified mediation programs elicited enhanced conflict management and problem-solving capacity from parties during unscripted aspects of mediation. In other words, there are certain parts of the mediation process that are scripted, prescribed, and rote in nature. However, most mediators will say that many successful outcomes start with nuances that aren't specifically spelled out. This is where mediator intuition appears to come into play. When parties are in conflict, the mediator often exhibits the ability to "read" the situation, emotion, and energy in the room to help steer parties to places they were unable to go to on their own (hence the need for mediation services in the first place). It was my hope that by studying this aspect of conflict management and examining these perspectives, my findings would create awareness and coping strategies to empower both the practitioner and participants to achieve even greater results.

There are many wonderful conflict management practitioners in the world, so determining whom to study was initially a quandary. Although I've emphasized here the need not to lean on self-preference when educating others, it was equally important to balance this with familiarity while navigating the research. I needed to ensure I understood the feedback gathered during the interview process. Because one of the primary areas my organization serves is agriculture, a critically important industry for the state of Iowa, it therefore seemed wise to use mediators tied to farming for continuity within the study. Across the country, forty-two of the fifty states possess federally designated mediation organizations certified by the USDA as solely authorized to offer agricultural mediations, though each of these entities also offers mediation services beyond the scope of agriculture.[13] There was enough consistency among the organizations and yet the practitioners also had a wide variety of experiences dealing with conflict. Using a selection process, I chose twenty experienced, certified mediators to participate in telephone interviews over the course of two weeks. Each participant was presented with the following four questions:

1. Describe the practices or skills you use during the unscripted aspects of mediation.

2. How do you elicit capacity in and among parties?

3. What is the relationship between the unscripted parts of mediation and your effectiveness in eliciting enhanced capacity in and among the parties?

4. What contexts or situations have influenced your experience or perspective regarding the unscripted aspects of mediation? What contexts or situations have influenced your experience or perspective with eliciting capacity among parties?

During the preparation process the participants were told the core concepts and terminology related to the study prior to the interviews. For example, the term "capacity," as it related to this study, meant the ability for parties to manage conflict through problem solving and creating viable solutions.

Depending on the breadth of information provided by the interviewees in the initial four questions, I presented the following three supplemental questions:

5. How do you assess the unscripted aspects that develop during mediations to determine the practices or skills you will utilize?

6. Describe a mediation case reflecting how you elicited capacity from parties during unscripted aspects/moments in the mediation.

7. What else would you like to share about your viewpoints on the unscripted aspects of mediation and capacity as it relates to your experiences as a mediator?

Unsure of what results I might get, I was delighted by the time and consideration each participant gave to thoughtfully answer these questions. Because every mediator was required to have at least five years of mediation experience to participate in the study, they provided a wealth of invaluable information. While the interviews were semi-structured, each participant was also provided the opportunity to openly share their insights and experiences regarding how they deal with the conflict management process. Because many of these mediators had other professional backgrounds prior to becoming mediators, many shared their involvement in conflict related to their previous work pursuits. Many also shared experiences from their personal lives as well. Their words were discerning and rich with nuggets of wisdom. To help map out the feedback provided by the participants, the information was coded using concept coding methodologies and resulted in seven thematic areas: Unscripted Actions, Unscripted Beliefs, Capacity Actions, Capacity Beliefs, Mediator Imagery, Mediator Background, and Mediator Motivation.

Seeing the seven areas of research come together was a rewarding process, because there was innate value in each topic. In fact, there is strong merit for studying each of the seven fields in the future. To best grow our understanding of conflict, however, I decided to narrow the focus to a singular area so it could be developed more fully. While the seven research outcomes are interesting, and each contributes to a better understanding of conflict management, I was particularly struck by the notion of mediator imagery. I kept having "Aha!" moments while reflecting on their feedback. Because it was revelatory and compelling to me, I trust it will be for others as well. Since when did images, imagination, and imagery play a role in conflict, and how do they help in the process of successfully managing it? This will be our journey in the coming chapters. I'm excited to have you join me.

Imagery Touchpoints:

1. How would you answer the seven research questions presented in this chapter? If you aren't a trained mediator, how do you think they answered these questions?

2. Why do you think the nuanced and instinctive aspects of conflict management haven't been studied in the same way the prescriptive areas have been? Why do you believe there is merit in understanding the more subjective parts of how to manage conflict?

3. What comes to your mind when you consider the terms imagery, images, and imagination? What do you think shaped your definition or perspective?

Imagery Snapshot: *The vantage point used during conflict definitely impacts outcomes. The focus of our lens shapes the information brought into view. Therefore, efforts to look to others inform us about how and why the conflict is evolving.*

How Imagery Introduced Itself

    Stan, one of the best mediators I know, happens to be a former plumber. His record as an exceptional mediator for more than thirty years is testament to the fact that great practitioners of conflict management can come from all walks of life. In fact, one could argue that his previous background as a plumber augmented his mediation abilities. His competence in his former role serves him well because typically plumbers are realistic, investigative, and process-oriented individuals.[14] They seek solutions to problems and are capable of remaining flexible while dealing with a variety of situations. If you ask me, these traits sound a lot like what we would expect to see in an individual skilled in conflict management. After all, conflict comes in all shapes and sizes. Handling conflict requires both nimbleness to navigate various scenarios and the pragmatism to reality test and create practical solutions.

    My organization has employed people from all walks of life who grew to become skilled mediators—a juvenile probation officer, a professor, a postmaster, a pastor, a route driver, a mechanic, an electrician, a chicken farmer, a social worker, a lawyer, a human resource manager, a teacher, a judge, a school counselor, and a banker. This is not a comprehensive list, but it serves to demonstrate the eclectic background of those who eventually embark on the mediation career path. We've hired people who were self-employed and those who worked for Fortune 500 companies before entering our small, non-profit doors. We've hired people with high school diplomas and those with doctorates. The point is that specific career paths or educational programs won't necessarily guarantee that you will be the world's best at managing conflict, nor that you will automatically struggle with conflict. That being said, certain personality types are drawn to careers and courses that lead them toward strong conflict management skills due to the natural characteristics required of the profession. However, I've also witnessed people pegged as good conflict managers based on their backgrounds, and they've fallen flat on their faces in the throes of disputes. The world of conflict is often complex, and it certainly isn't linear or scripted. We shouldn't assume any unilateral formula or path to be the source for recruiting the ideal conflict manager. Wonderful practitioners spring from many wells.

As I mentioned, I approached my first mediation with far too much confidence, so I intentionally ate humble pie and swung the other way with my dissertation research. I decided to admit to a level of cluelessness about what the research process would reveal. I was fairly certain that all of the participants would extol the wonders of mediation because this work is nothing short of brilliant. Beyond that, however, the research feedback was a blank slate. All kidding aside, I do hope people working in a professional capacity enjoy their chosen field. Not everyone has the luxury of working in jobs they like, but one can hope. For me, I found the world of mediation and conflict management to be one of the greatest enrichments of my life and a deeply rewarding career. I digress, but this is my shout-out to this quiet profession that does so much good for the world!

Back to the topic at hand, the research participants and their feedback. Because an open-ended format was used to allow the participants to organically share their thoughts, I wasn't sure what common threads might unfold. All interviews were intentionally conducted over a two-week window in order to connect the dots with any patterns they might reveal. While the participants were asked to provide a mediation scenario demonstrating how they had developed the conflict management and problem-solving capacity among parties during the unscripted aspects of mediation, no one was asked to provide examples or scenarios outside of their mediation experiences. (See reference question six from the interview survey found in chapter two.) But to my surprise, every single interview had at least one reference to an outside example. Some provided multiple insights into their worlds apart from professional conflict management. In fact, many of the interviewees would even make comments like, "I am not sure if this is relevant to your study, but I remember a time in my childhood when I..." or, "I don't know if this pertains to my mediation skills, but my wife tells me I often..." or, "I know this isn't a mediation example, but I remember in my last job when I..."

After recording, compiling, and transcribing all of the interviews, I started contemplating the pattern. Because each of these individuals had a wealth of direct experience with conflict management, they could have provided information from their professional mediation lives. Each person knew I was a seasoned mediator, so it wasn't like they thought I might not have a full understanding of their work responsibilities. They knew I wouldn't be confused by any jargon or concepts related to the mediation field as I am currently an active practitioner myself. Yet each had offered extraprofessional illustrations to more accurately describe professional experiences. It was a captivating revelation. They were providing insights, wisdom, and perspectives that transcended their work, almost as if they were saying, "I offer great skills as a mediator and practitioner in conflict management, but my skills didn't grow from my professional background. The seeds were planted outside of my business identity. You can't separate one from the other and fully understand why I'm good at what I do. I am able to navigate the world of conflict management because I tap into all that I am to best inform my practice. Pay attention to this because it helps reveal why some mediators are so adept at helping people work their way through conflict."

So I decided to pay attention. One notable interview with an individual named Mike really helped me tap into the cues the participants were providing. When I asked this mediator, who was also an attorney, what he does to elicit capacity among disputing parties, he paused for a moment.

"Many people today would be too young to know why this example is impactful to me," he said finally, "but I'm going to tell you anyway as it helped me a great deal when I was learning about mediation. Someone once told me that to be skilled with conflict, you need to view the situation like Wayne Gretzky. He doesn't skate *to* the puck. He skates to where the puck is *going* to be. Addressing conflict requires a lot of anticipation about what might come next. So, to me, I need to be Wayne Gretzky when I help people in disputes."

What resonated with me was two-fold. One, he understood that if I didn't know who Wayne Gretzky was that the example wouldn't be as meaningful, and two, he decided that a mental illustration related to hockey better served his feedback than merely telling me that a good mediator needs to have the ability to anticipate.[15] Side note: Mike is absolutely correct that the world needs more Wayne Gretzky types in the conflict hockey rink.

I found it just as interesting that Mike had taken a long pause before offering his example. At first, I thought he might be pausing because he was unsure whether he should give an example outside of professional experiences since he hadn't been asked for one. However, as I conducted more interviews and studied more transcripts, I began to draw a different conclusion. Every single person paused prior to providing the example and point of reference for what they lean on to guide their conflict management skills. I believe the pause came because the participants were slowing themselves down for a momentary reflection to consider what they naturally draw upon to be good practitioners. They didn't spew a laundry list of conventional steps and processes related to mediation, nothing ready-made or prepared, as some experts might do. Instead, they broadened their reflections and shared a deeper sense of how they developed and utilized their organic, authentic mediation skills.

This leads to another observation. Successful practitioners of conflict management know the importance of self-reflection, drawing upon holistic experiences to shape their skills and not just painting by the numbers when dealing with the human condition. I call this the "why-to-the-what" phenomenon. Essentially, to know how to do the *what* of something, the person should understand the *why* of it. Basically, this is my paraphrased version of the adage, "give a man a fish and you feed him for a day; teach him to fish, and you feed him for a lifetime." But there's more than one way to catch a fish. I'm no fishing expert, but my brother's an avid outdoorsman, and I know enough to understand that people can cast a rod-and-reel, fly fish, spear fish, ice fish, or cast gill nets. (I've watched a few too many survival television shows in my day, which is why I admittedly know what a gill net is.) Let's just chalk this up to my attempt at being a good sister and trying to have a wider background from which to draw upon for survival in the jungle of life's conflicts.

One reason the metaphor about fishing has stood the test of time is because there are multiple ways that a person can catch a fish, and fishing is done around the world in rivers, ponds, seas, and oceans. In fact, there are at least 33 identified types of fishing styles![16] If there was only one method that worked or one place in the world where people fished, this metaphor would likely be too rigid or difficult to understand to enter into "old adage" status. The fact that people can visualize how *they* would fish—the fact that a variety of fresh and saline bodies of water *can* be fished—is what makes the saying relevant to a broad audience. It allows people to create their own illustrations. Go fish in a pond, lake, river, sea, or ocean to see how these different forms of water have transcendental commonalities.

Similarly, though the core topic was conflict management, I believe a variety of examples were provided by the interviewees because people picture themselves dealing with conflict in different ways that they find natural to them. It would be helpful if a person had actually fished before to truly appreciate the fishing metaphor, but it isn't required. The same goes with the Wayne Gretzky example. It might be helpful to have played hockey to get a full sense of the metaphor, but it isn't necessary. This is why Mike provided the example even after stating that some people might be too young to know the player—he had enough wisdom to understand that people would identify with his overarching representation. The key is to provide an illustration that has enough universal appeal to be understood and embraced by the audience.

To that end, I decided that another aspect related to Mike's response needed to be considered. What would happen if the hockey example was used with someone who had never seen a hockey match at all? What would happen if the fishing example was used with someone who had never witnessed fishing or ever eaten fish? Would the impact from those imagery statements be as effective or profound?

Can deep meaning about complex, abstract concepts using concrete illustrations be conveyed if the audience can't relate to the illustrations? Perhaps this is why children struggle to understand foreign proverbs that are taught during their formative education. Maybe this is why so many children's books use pictures and colors to amplify the words of the author and why some authors enjoy doing both the illustrations and the writing. It allows them the control to connect abstract messages with concrete images. This is likely why the art found in children's books has changed over time.[17] Just look at the library books you checked out as a small child compared to the picture books sold today for parents to read to their children. To best connect with the young reader, the illustrator needs to create something that connects with the changing eye of each new generation learning to read. While I'm not an early childhood educator, I assume that using pictures relevant to the reader helps accelerate their understanding of the words on the page. This is also why cartoons, pictographs, and paintings have been around since time immemorial, and why they will likely continue to exist and evolve. Pictures, whether printed on a paper or scratched into a cave wall, convey a story. And alongside text, they aid in the comprehension of complicated lessons and explanations.

It's a safe bet that cookbooks with detailed and beautiful pictures associated with the recipes sell better than text-only cookbooks. The recipes could be exactly the same, but a person might breeze right past the cookbooks that don't contain pictures.[18] People often buy these types of books to learn new techniques and tips alongside the recipes, so it makes sense that audiences would appreciate pictures to help boost their understanding of what the end product should look like. They are exploring an area of cooking novel to them. Go to your own kitchen and see which of your cookbooks speak the most to you. Are there pages that jump out more than others? Do the cookbooks with pictures create more motivation and confidence to try the recipes? I must admit, I'm still trying to decide whether I'm brave enough to master the art of baking a Grand Marnier soufflé. Not to toot my own horn, but I am second-to-none at devouring these beautiful soufflés. It's a gift.

Imagery Touchpoints:

1. Have you ever been in a situation where a person used a word you didn't know? How did you respond or deal with the lack of information? What did your confusion do for the way you processed the words?

2. What types of hobbies or tasks do you undertake where you typically look for pictures to help aid your comprehension of what you're reading?

3. Do you use metaphors or quotes to drive home a point when talking to people? Which do you use, or which do you hear other people use in conversation? Why do you think these specific examples are utilized rather than others?

Imagery Snapshot: *Metaphors create the opportunity for reflection and understanding through poetic imagery. Anecdotes essentially serve as miniature stories to help people more quickly understand the simplified plotline for something that might otherwise be abstract or complex.*

Instruction Manual on Conflict

Have you ever noticed that many instruction manuals are tossed aside?[19] That's why there are people who avoid ordering products with "some assembly required." Nothing is more frustrating than opening up a box containing your highly anticipated piece of furniture only to discover there are five million screws that must be attached to three million different holes found on eight million parts of the wooden boards. I don't know about you, Dr. Jekyll, but this brings out my Mr. Hyde. I'd rather go to the dentist every day for a week to get a root canal than be subject to the pain and misery of trying to digest an instruction manual. It's like I get an internal version of road-rage when I have to assemble something requiring directions. Maybe the phrase "assembly-rage" should be coined to describe my loathing. It's not like I'm incapable of following directions and building prefabricated things—I can pass a college statistics class (with a *lot* of tears and perseverance)—but I navigate an instruction manual the same way I steer down a highway with road construction. I grit my teeth because there's something inherently maddening when hic-cups and challenges arise in either of these settings. Admittedly, these situations tend to bring out the worst in me. Road-rage and assem-bly-rage aren't my best modes of self-expression. Just ask my kids.

In recent years, however, my assembly-rage has diminished a great deal. I've discovered this brilliant tool called the internet. It allows me to type in what I'm trying to learn about, and voila! A video magically appears! I can watch the experts put something together in three minutes that would have taken me three hours. In fact, I've now come to accept the house-ownership challenges that often pop up with a certain degree of glee. I no longer believe my house is going to outwit me. By golly, I will assemble that piece of furniture, fix that broken toilet seat, and entirely rewire my knob-and-tube electrical wiring. (Whoa! Let's not go that far, Ms. HGTV! And no, there isn't any knob-and-tube wiring in my house for all those concerned for my personal safety. Don't tattle on me to the local home inspector.) In the interest of transparency, I might have a secret obsession with home repair television shows that give me too much self-assurance in my contractor skills. Case in point, a recessed light recently went kaput toward the end of the evening, and because I lack almost any degree of rational patience, I decided that waiting until the morning for an electrician wasn't a sensible decision. Enter my trusty best friend, the internet. We spent a few heartfelt moments together, and my kindly internet shared a variety of videos on the topic. That's what BFFs do. We share with each other. I'm fairly cer-tain Bob Vila was proud that night, as my light is still shining brightly today.

The videos found on the internet seem to empower me far more than a simple written pamphlet of instructions on the same topic. Unless the pictures are insanely good, and they usually aren't. The words could be exactly the same on the video and in the pamphlet, but the impact isn't as rich with only the written word. Amplifying the instructions with movement, color, and audio helps me better understand what the instructor is trying to convey. I can usually comprehend and more efficiently engage with the materials when more of my senses are activated. Due to the success of platforms like YouTube, I'm fairly confident I'm not alone in this assessment. People tend to internalize and embrace complexities better when more holistic tools are provided to them. No one wants to be given the task of building a bookshelf with only a hammer in their tool belt. The same can be said for learning about best practices associated with conflict management. Most people don't want a scripted textbook with bullet points to help them learn such a complicated topic. Mapping this out through various personal examples and connections is a solid way to create meaning about the unscripted, complex, and abstract aspects of conflict management.

At this point, you might be asking yourself why you bought this book in the first place when I seemingly just trashed instructions that are only in writing. No worries, dear reader. We will be getting to visual aids later in the book as I believe they have a place in the learning process. It's also equally important to highlight that this book is not an instruction manual. We are embarking on an illustrative journey where our imagery can be captured through the written and visual world. Illustrations of the mind develop through a variety of channels if they are constructively formed. For now, let's lay the backdrop about imagery and conflict so we can later use visual cues and models to elevate our understanding. Additionally, questions are included at the end of each chapter to help with personal reflection before moving on in the material. I promise that very soon we will be shifting to the practical applications of the journey in better mastering the skills and perspectives useful for assisting others in conflict.

Before we head that direction, let's expand upon the examples that the twenty mediators provided to me during my dissertation interviews. Remember, seven thematic areas emerged from the initial study: Unscripted Actions, Unscripted Beliefs, Capacity Actions, Capacity Beliefs, Mediator Imagery, Mediator Background, and Mediator Motivation. In a nutshell, the first four themes had to do with the actions and beliefs these participants felt were necessary to help people successfully deal with conflict. This was the part of the study where participants shared that the keys to mediation success were the power of nuanced observation, using instinct, paying attention to subtle cues, and focusing on the undercurrent of conflict. The practitioners described these as a natural state of being for them. It was difficult for them to articulate and fully describe these finessed aspects of the mediation process, but they could express how critically important they were to success during conflict management.

As a trainer who believes in the importance of the "why-to-the-what" process, it wasn't enough to tell people that the aspects sitting below the surface of conflict are as important, if not more, than the aspects right in front of them without helping them first understand the "whys" involved. To guide those who wished to tap their conflict management abilities, I needed to help create a path for people to understand their personal "why" so they could turn around and implement the "what" into their practice. This is where the fifth theme of the study emerged: Mediator Imagery.

As previously noted, every participant in my dissertation study provided unprompted examples about how their skills developed from areas outside of their professional realm. In fact, I identified eighteen overarching themes: nature, music, travel, theater, construction, art, games, food, medicine, weddings, school, sports, animals, dance, technology, clothing, shopping, and dating. Obviously, these examples aren't part of the professional narrative for a mediator unless they happen to also be teachers, photographers, doctors, or chefs. This isn't to say that none of these practitioners had previous work experiences outside of professional mediation, but only that at that moment, none held jobs outside of the field of conflict management. However, this didn't prevent them from providing examples that clearly fell outside of the role of a mediator, and this is what made their illustrations particularly insightful. The fact that they felt compelled to draw upon areas outside of their work functions showed the importance of having a depth of understanding and a holistic approach to conflict. Additionally, it is notable that the examples they gave were often very positive in nature. Some might find it ironic that people involved in conflict, typically a topic with negative connotations, might use cheerful, colorful, and encouraging examples to create illustrative models about what has informed their mediation and conflict management practices. In the table on the next page, you can see how I grouped these themes together according to the types of phrases and anecdotes they gave. A pretty creative and bright group if you ask me!

Many of the practitioners used commonly understood cultural components of living in America, like sports, art, music, and food. Some even went as far as to site specific examples to support their views, like the throwback to *The Wizard of Oz* and the game of Twenty Questions. I especially appreciated the reference to our great American pastime, baseball. If we are honest with ourselves, aren't there times when it feels like fastballs are being thrown at us when we have to deal with conflict? Stepping up to the plate is half the battle.

THEME	IMAGERY CONCEPTS GIVEN BY THE MEDIATORS (paraphrased)
Animals	• People are like animals who want their basic needs met. • Be the chameleon in the room. • Not my circus; Not my monkeys is the guiding principle of mediation.
Art	• People will be colorful and sometimes color outside the lines. • It's an art and it's an activity. • Know your medium. Are you working with charcoal, watercolors, canvas, wood, or metal? • We are crafting when we mediate.
Clothing	• Conflict is like getting dressed. There are many options for clothing, colors, and styles. • Ask people to take their mask off to show they are human.
Construction	• Build your own dream; build your own future. • We are the bridge. • Build a bridge.
Dance	• It's like a dance; it's like the waltz. One person makes a move and the other person makes a counter move.
Dating	• Conflict is like dating. There is a back-and-forth and it's often hard to imagine the break-up and a life without it.
Food	• It's like cooking from scratch. It's never exactly the same recipe. • Not everything fits into a mold. • It's like an onion with many layers.
Games	• It's a game of connect-the-dots. • It is the game of Twenty Questions. • People are likes puzzles; we are tasked with figuring out the pieces.

THEME	IMAGERY CONCEPTS GIVEN BY THE MEDIATORS (paraphrased)
Medicine	• It's like going to the doctor's office with a rash. You know there is a rash. You don't need to be told there is a rash. You need options to treat the rash and prevent it from returning.
Music	• Treat mediation like jazz – improvisation. • Mediation is like music where there is a need for command of the basic scales. Then you move to the variation. • Dealing with conflict is like an accordion that moves in and out flexibly. • Mediation is like jazz where there is tremendous room for improvisation and variance within set tolerances and boundaries. • Like jazz, there is a general sequence, solos, and playing together in mediation.
Nature	• It's like gardening where we need to plant seeds. • There will be a different landscape if conflict is settled.
School	• Dealing with conflict during mediation is like the rules on the kindergarten board. • Conflict ground rules are like the rules that kids use on playgrounds. • Mediation is like teaching and we are essentially tutors. • It's like learning math where basic algorithms are used and then you move to other formulas.
Shopping	• It's like real estate: Buyer's remorse; change in ownership; exhaustion from all the options. A lot of time is spent looking for houses, and once the decision is made the options are no longer there.

THEME	IMAGERY CONCEPTS GIVEN BY THE MEDIATORS (paraphrased)
Sports	• Follow the Wayne Gretzky model of not skating to where the puck is but where the puck is going to be. • Be a poker player so you are unflappable and keep up with the cards played. • Mediation is like asking a professional baseball player how they throw 100mph. They can explain some parts and others just happen. Some layers are based on knowledge, thinking, and experience. Other parts operate below the conscious level. • Conflict is like boxing. There are the elements of fighting, intensity, politeness. Eventually the gloves are taken down or put away.
Technology	• There are a bunch of wires going out, and you're trying to see which ones make the electrical connection with the other person.
Theater	• Mediators are directors in a play that has some improvisation. • Set the stage. • It's like a soap opera where the program is full of surprises and the best and worst of human drama. • It's the *Wizard of Oz* with no markers on the road or a perfect fork in the road. The yellow brick road might have broken stones, missing stones, demons, flying monkeys causing problems. It isn't a clean road.
Travel	• Go where the road takes you. Sometimes it will lead to a dead end and other times you find the best path. • Mediation explores pathways where different courses are discovered.
Weddings	• It's like a wedding where the orientation is the dress-rehearsal and the mediation is the recital.

Imagery Touchpoints:

1. Have you ever used the internet to learn how to make or fix something? Is there a recipe, home improvement task, or car repair you felt confident to approach after using an online video or tutorial?

2. Is there a time when you were taught the "what" of the task without understanding the "why"? How did it impact your speed at learning that task? How did it impact your willingness to integrate the lesson into your life?

3. Looking at the Imagery Concept table, are there certain themes, examples, or phrases that resonate with you? What is it about them that connects for you?

Imagery Snapshot: *Identifying your personal conflict imagery template develops your toolbox **and** your manual by adding one more set of skills to build confidence and proficiency.*

The Maze of Conflict Confusion

Caucus. It's a word frequently used in my world. For Iowans, it describes the process during presidential elections to get a pulse on how people feel about possible political candidates.[20] For mediators, it describes the process when private meetings are used during sessions so people can confidentially share their views.[21] For people outside of Iowa or the mediation profession, however, the word "caucus" probably carries little weight. So I was surprised when during a meeting I attended, an Iowa mediator used the word with an audience filled with non-mediators from all over the United States. It only took me a moment to realize that the word had little meaning for the group. Thankfully, I picked up on the energy from the partic-ipants and provided a quick definition of the word so we could move forward with a meaningful discussion.

Most of the examples from the dissertation survey were ones I clearly understood. I could internalize the concepts they were trying to articulate. Other concepts, however, weren't so clear to me. For instance, the real estate example didn't resonate with me. The person shared that helping people navigate conflict is like the exhausting process of digging through a plethora of housing choices. Then comes the long negotiation where, only if the process is successful, eventually the buyer owns a home. What confused me, though, was her last statement. She shared that after the home sale closes, the buyer no longer has options. The buyer went from looking at many houses to eventually choosing just one home. She indicated that this can lead to buyer's remorse or even a sense of panic that options are no longer available. I can't relate to this because I've loved every home I've owned—four to date. Even after getting divorced and having to find a home on my own with three young children to provide for, I was relieved when I found one.

For me, a house is just a structure; what I do with it makes it a home. I get to create the dwelling space. That's why people will be greeted with bright walls, eclectic décor, and painted furniture when they come visit me. I set the tone for my guests through the vibrant, diverse, and random ways I infuse my personality into my home. I understand that people can have buyer's remorse and feel a loss due to fewer options, but I feel otherwise. I believe the options change, and I *get* to tackle any homeownership challenges that could other-wise create buyer's remorse. Now I have freedom. I get to shift gears and be in control again. So on one hand, I can relate to her real estate example and how it pertains to conflict, but on the other, I still view mediation and conflict management as the process of creating solu-tions that pass the baton over to the "buyer." From there, they get to craft their new, hopefully improved, future. Even if the outcome of the conflict management process wasn't exactly what they desired, as is often the case when we compromise, they were involved in the negotiation process, and now they know how to move forward. The options have simply changed.

Today, when I read through the list of examples provided by the mediators, I still don't easily connect with the post-home-buying concerns in the real estate scenario. This isn't to say she's wrong—maybe she's had different experiences with real estate—but because I've never been a realtor and haven't owned that many properties, maybe I'm out of touch with the situation she describes. Maybe her perception is closer to what the majority of homeowners feel. Nonetheless, it doesn't jive as naturally with me as some of the other examples do, so I tend to gloss over it when I read the table I've provided in chapter four. We all have an initial inclination to skim past whatever is too complicated, detached, or impersonal for our minds to process. If it requires us to flex our thinking, we often jump over to our areas of comfort. Go back and read the list in the table from the previous chapter. See whether you spend more time on the examples that connect with you. I don't think this is a reflection of laziness but rather a way for people to be efficient. There is so much information and stimulation in the world that editing down is the fastest and surest way to insulate and increase survival.

Could the same be true of conflict? When we get into a dispute with others, there is a natural propensity to home in on what *I* want, what *I* know, what *I* perceive. Who I am and what I'm naturally drawn to shapes my approach to conflict. Should I feel badly that I can't entirely relate to the real-estate scenario? Or should I graciously understand that my perspective is honed by what has touched me directly? Similarly, her vantage point is a conglomeration of the experiences and beliefs she holds dear. There's enough room in the universe for varying perspectives on all matters, especially those of the spirit that are particularly complex. Perhaps nothing is more complex than trying to tread the waters of conflict when the undercurrent is strong and the lifeboat doesn't seem to be readily in sight.

See how I used a swimming metaphor to explain my position?

I realize I run the risk that not everyone reading the book will appreciate it, but hopefully it's broad enough for people to understand my intent. The point is that we use imagery, illustrations, and imagination all the time to connect our inner ideas to the outside world. The key, however, is figuring out how to best use these tools to make connections in the most impactful way while still honoring our internal voice and style.

Recently, I was talking to my kids and trying to describe the personality of someone they hadn't met, and I used the analogy "busy bee" to help them understand the frenetic nature of the person. My youngest son didn't get the message I was trying to communicate and asked what it meant. My older son was able to tell him that if someone is a "busy bee," they are constantly in motion, like a bee buzzing from flower to flower. I was tickled that he was teaching his brother because my younger son was understanding his older brother. My middle daughter's eyes grew wide, and she said, "I'm glad to learn what this meant. I was worried you were describing the person as really mean."

I was perplexed, so I asked her about her thought process. She explained to the family that her experience with a bee was it stinging her, so she assumed the phrase "busy bee" meant stinging a lot of people. My goodness! Teaching failure on my part. Had my younger son not asked what my example meant, my daughter would have had a very different image of the person than I intended. I made an assumption about my kids' level of understanding and their experience with this insect and the colloquialism "busy bee." I thought it was an excellent way to illustrate the temperament of the person. Alas, I'd simply created confusion. One child had fully understood the example, one didn't completely get it, and another misunderstood it altogether.

While failing to create an illustration that all three of my kids could follow, it was a wonderful teaching opportunity—for *me*, that is. If we don't check in to ensure people understand our use of imagery, we risk that they might not understand our message, or worse yet, they might inadvertently misconstrue it. Is it their job to inform us they don't understand the illustration or to inform us how they mentally map it out? Or is it *our* job to occasionally check in to ensure we are painting a picture they can follow? I'm curious how often we try to communicate something abstract or hidden within ourselves through literal means that don't resonate with people the same way they do for us. Busy Bee, meet Realtor.

It would be wonderful if I could say that the example with my kids is uncommon, but I don't believe that's true. I thought back to my childhood and distinctly remember a time when I was so glad the teacher didn't call on me during a lesson when my hand was confidently raised. She had written the word "peasant" on the board and asked if anyone knew what the word meant. She had written only the word; it was our job to read it on our own and give a definition. My arm shot into the air, but to my disappointment, she called on another know-it-all student who told the class that peasant described someone who was poor.

"What an idiot," I thought to myself. "Everyone knows a peasant is a bird. DUH!" Except I was the only little student who had inserted an "H" into the word in her mind, spelling "pheasant" instead. As a child of an avid hunter, I was picturing myself gleefully trailing after my dad out hunting the fields of Iowa. News flash: peasant and pheasant do not mean the same thing. It was a shocking revelation to this elementary student.

No wonder the world of conflict can be so confusing. If a concept as simple as "busy bee" can go haywire and the word "peasant" can be mentally misspelled, why wouldn't very complicated and intense matters related to conflict be even more of a maze? Point of reference has a massive impact on perception. Context matters, and internal context *really* matters. In other words, the internal scripts within ourselves often act as tipping points for how and why we behave in certain ways. Most of the time, we operate so efficiently that we may not even be aware that these internal forces are guiding our steps. In fact, without a mindful and deliberate method to reflect on our chosen behaviors and decisions, we could coast through life without ever checking in to explore our minds and identify what might be shaping our decisions and direction in life.

Mindfulness appears to be a popular trend right now, and some people roll their eyes when something is presented as psychobabble. However, mindfulness is an ancient practice found in many cultures where an individual decides to focus their awareness in a particular area.[22] For food-lovers out there, think of mindfulness as the attempt at really appreciating a meal. Instead of eating your food on the couch while watching Netflix (no judgement, however, for enjoying this method of food consumption), imagine how you would savor a special, celebratory birthday dinner. You are sitting at the dining room table with your favorite meal and a glass of fine wine. The meal is served on nice dinnerware, and the only source of light is a candle. This allows you to focus on the meal. You aren't distracted by anything else around you. You are able take your time and smell the delicious food, swirl the wine in a lovely crystal goblet, and slowly cut the meal into bites and savor them. The food and beverage eventually get consumed and end up as nourishment, just as they would if the meal was inhaled on paper plates. However, the experience is radically different from that of a TV dinner.

The same goes for our approach to understanding what guides our behavior and decisions related to conflict. Conflict will pop up regardless of whether we decide to be mindful about it. The experience is drastically different, however, when we make the decision to learn how our internal and external worlds interact to impact our values, beliefs, perceptions, actions, decisions, and behaviors regarding conflict. Mindfulness is simply an avenue by which we learn how our internal state informs our external state. Once we understand our individual conflict DNA, we can then utilize this information to become better practitioners and educators of conflict management.

As a quick science recap (thank you Biochemistry 101), DNA is a central carrier of information.[23] It is the informer on life. It conveys the good, the bad, the beautiful, and the ugly in the world. When natural order is followed, harmony exists. Picture it this way: a perfect strawberry on a hot summer day. When mismatches or errors occur, mutations will result. Another picture: terminal cancer that stifles a beloved's final breath. When we home in on DNA, we increase the ability to deal with potential mutations sooner rather than later. Doing so also increases the likelihood of generating better outcomes, like that idyllic strawberry. Internal observations at the micro level have a huge ability to create great external tangibles. Just because DNA can't be seen with the naked eye doesn't mean it doesn't exist. Likewise, just because our internal universe and what has influenced it isn't necessarily observable to others doesn't mean it's any less relevant. In fact, just like DNA, the micro-universe has a huge hand in how the world unfolds around us.

For the Bible readers in the audience, it's perhaps no coincidence that Jesus references the mustard seed when describing faith in Mark 4:30-32. These seeds are tiny. However, in ideal conditions, these plants can grow thirty feet tall. For a bush, that is no small feat. It's amazing that something so small, buried in the earth, can grow to astounding heights with the proper soil, nutrients, sun, and water. Considering this species is native to the Middle East and not the United States, it should come as no surprise that most Americans would need to research what the mustard plant looks like when fully grown. Admittedly, I had to search the internet to find pictures of this mysterious mustard plant.[24] Because it grows wild in the area where Jesus lived, it now makes sense why this example would have resonated so clearly with the people to whom he was preaching. Check it out for yourself, and you'll find that it's a remarkable plant. Then I bet you'll have a different appreciation for the phrase "faith like a mustard seed" the next time you hear it. Better yet, you can now play the scholar when you find yourself among theological types playing a game of Trivial Pursuit.

Faith like a mustard seed. Jesus understood that faith is an internal construct that could be hard for people to grasp without an external image with which to associate it. Because his followers would readily be exposed to both the mustard seed and the mustard plant, he used a great illustration to help make his point. For those wishing to explore ancient illustrations, the Bible is replete with them. One of the easiest ways to study this is to spend a few moments in the Book of Matthew:

1. Can a camel go through an eye of a needle? Of course not. This illustration was used to explain the downside of unmanaged wealth. (Matthew 19:20)

2. Do lily flowers sweat about how they will grow? That's absurd. This imagery was used to teach about worry and anxiety. (Matthew 6:28-30)

3. Are human beings used as lamps in homes? Duh. This analogy was used to demonstrate how to be a good role model to the world. (Matthew 5:14-16)

A bit of investigation reveals that camels, lilies, and oil lamps were commonly found throughout much of the Middle East and Africa. Matthew was no dummy when he recorded these parables shared by

Jesus to the listening crowds. He clearly understood the fundamental teaching principle of making sure the learner had mental depictions to connect the unseen with the seen. If you can visualize it, you will probably understand it in a more meaningful and enduring way.

Another case in point: being called "salty" is a modern slang expression for someone difficult or irritated. However, many believe the origin of this expression also stems from the Bible. The book of Matthew comes into play here once again. It's the example used when Jesus describes the importance of people being like salt. He knew that everyone at that time used salt as a method of seasoning. Too much is a bad thing. Too little is a bad thing. Salt is an avenue to augment and complement when it is used with a balanced hand. The way the phrase is used today, being salty is when too much intensity or attitude is brought to a situation. Whether a person is reading the Bible or the Urban Dictionary, the use of the word salt tells a story.[25] This mineral seasoning is universally valued, so pass the salt please, and don't be salty about it!

Imagery Touchpoints:

1. Have you ever been in a classroom or training environment where the instructor used an example or an expression with which you were unfamiliar? How did you deal with this situation? What did it do for your experience?

2. How do you best define mindfulness for yourself? The analogy of DNA was provided in this chapter, yet you may have a more insightful example for yourself. If something evokes curiosity within you, that's a good starting point for shaping your mindfulness philosophy.

3. Look around your favorite room in your home. What items are you surrounded by that mean something to you? Find an item that a stranger wouldn't appreciate the way you do. How would you go about explaining the meaning of the item to them?

Imagery Snapshot: *Familiarity establishes context and meaning for what follows. We are designed to be efficient creatures, so anything that becomes normalized is what we comfortably retrieve in new situations.*

Conflict Imagery Comes to Life

The first part of this book provides a variety of examples that shed light on how people use imagery, illustration, and imagination to help express themselves. It's a cornerstone of the human condition. What my dissertation research unveiled is the frequency with which imagery is used and how it is regularly done subconsciously. When asked what had formalized and shaped their mediation practices, a large number of participants didn't initially offer any specific examples. However, at some point during the interview, *every* participant offered an illustrative representation of their mediation beliefs, behaviors, or practices. It was almost innate for each individual to give an image to help better describe themselves as conflict management practitioners. This discovery is why I decided to write this book. I felt an obligation to inform the world about my piece of enlightenment. I can now say the following concepts with confidence: Everyone will encounter conflict at some point. People behave and make choices based on their specific experience with conflict, and individuals demonstrate external behaviors that are influenced by their internal state. People develop their imaginations through internal image associations, and they frequently use this imagery during communication with others.

I could teach about my philosophies and beliefs on conflict management, and you would glean some useful nuggets of wisdom. However, you are the best teacher of your own approach to conflict management. I could share how being born without full hearing and battling auditory surgeries throughout my childhood has impacted my fierce perspective on advocacy and ensuring people are heard during conflict. You probably wouldn't be surprised to learn how this significant hearing impairment has influenced my views on communication, and we all know that communication is directly tied to conflict management. I could have written that detail into my introduction to this book. I could have also told you about how my dad died from suicide when I was fourteen, and that I moved and attended two schools through my high school career, effectively splitting my high school experience in half. You can understand how these experiences have affected my relationships with people, my views about trust, and the deep value I place on self-reliance. Further, I could tell you about living in three different states, attending three different colleges, being married and divorced over the span of twenty years, bearing three children within a three-year period, serving as a director of a state-wide nonprofit, being a sister (and middle child) of two brothers, being a daughter, being an avid long distance runner, being a wannabe DIYer of all things crafty, being a word-junkie and an absolute math-hater, and feeling blessed to have so many loyal friends.

What would this accomplish, though? You would have a highlight (and lowlight) reel from the biography of my life. It would help create understanding about how *my* views on the world were shaped. You would get a sense for what triggers me and how I interpret conflict when it presents itself. These are useful starting points when teaching others to think about their approach to conflict because they demonstrate the events that have informed my conflict management practice. It helps create imagery for you to connect my external conflict management framework with my internal state of being. However, the heavy lifting comes when *you* reflect upon *your* life and internal state to create *your* own narrative for *your* own conflict management system. This is why one-size-fits-all just simply doesn't work with conflict management. This is why conflict has remained a topic of conversation since time immemorial. Experts can shed light on generalities and best practices, but essentially, it comes down to how you best navigate conflict given who you are as an individual. Using the analogy of a boat, if the mind is the vessel, then only you can serve as its captain. Maps, instructions, and equipment are here as guideposts, but only the captain has the capacity to physically set sail on that sea. For my driving folks, think of your mind as your "ride or die." Like it or not, your mind sticks with you to the very end. As such, you might as well use it to drive the conflict roads in front of you.

The Imagery Approach to Conflict Management, the model presented in upcoming chapters, was created to bridge the gap in conflict management practices between the self-identification of internal imagery and personal conflict management scripts. Rule-based prescriptions about the dos and don'ts of managing conflict are already available, but these best practices can only carry people so far. This is why many of the supervisory, leadership, communication, and conflict training sessions available only shed light on the external aspects related to these topics. The shortcoming is that they fail to clearly depict what truly enlightens, informs, and shapes these external components. I believe this gap exists simply because it's hard to articulate the internal, unscripted, nuanced, and finessed parts of the world. The instinctive, gut facets of our existence are highly personal and often too nebulous to articulate succinctly to others.

Great leaders, mediators, experts, and conflict negotiators know how to draw the best from within themselves, and in turn draw the best from others, through mindfully understanding that who they are as individuals isn't who others are. They don't expect others to be a mirror of themselves. They don't try to take their hat off and put it on others. Instead, they use their hat to help others find their own, so they can dress themselves. (See that old adage about fishing.) When everyone wears their own hat, the authentic process of conflict management becomes ripe for genuinely successful outcomes. The dualism in scenarios of "I'm right, you're wrong" or "My method is superior; yours is inferior" starts to dissipate when we begin to realize that life isn't neat and tidy. Everything isn't always black and white. Gray exists, especially when it pertains to conflict and managing people who are hoping to achieve positive outcomes. If confronting conflict was absolute and simple, then fights at recess, divorces, cyber-bullying, failed business ventures, broken friendships, political smear campaigns, and world wars would cease to exist. Navigating life as though it should always manifest as a pretty little bow is naïve at best.

Because I'm aware that no magic wand exists regarding conflict management, the Imagery Approach to Conflict Management was created to shed more light on this complicated topic. It is my humble, yet inspired and passionate attempt at helping you inwardly reflect on the internal, abstract, unscripted parts of your being that can help you become adept at the art of managing conflict in others and within yourself. And I truly believe self-conflict-management is a much steeper hike than helping others. Both mountains, however, are scalable, and the views from the top can be unbelievably enlightening and empowering. The process begins by deciding that the trek toward the summit is worth the effort and that whatever terrain you stumble upon is worth discovering.

Below is a visual aid to help graphically symbolize the Imagery Approach to Conflict Management. I was fortunate enough to have a good friend and gifted graphic designer, Jen, help with this model. In her own right, she demonstrated skills similar to those of a conflict manager, bringing my internal vision to life in a concrete way. The goal was a one-page snapshot that visually represents the importance of bridging our external/tangible conflict management style with our internal/intangible personal environment. You will hear me use external/tangible and internal/intangible interchangeably with the terms concrete and abstract. I do so because the words concrete and abstract can be somewhat academic and stuffy in nature. Therefore, I use as many descriptive words as possible to help you connect with whatever words or phrases hold the most meaning to you. Better yet, feel free to use your own words or phrases to drive home the point. All I am asking is that each of us discovers or creates our own unique imagery to help illicit the imagination and creativity that resides within each one of us. That's how we create our own conflict management approach.

Take time to study the model and let it marinate for a bit to see and feel what unfolds for you personally. Once you have reviewed the model, move on to the next chapter for self-discovery work to trace how individual conflict development, tipping points, and outlooks are shaped.

The best way to move beyond dualism on any complicated topic is to try to unearth the roots that feed it. It's harder to remain in a dualistic mindset when insights are gathered that show how a more holistic approach can provide better clarity. Later, I'll show you how I put this model into practice while training a group of farmers. As a self-admitted city slicker living in a predominantly agricultural state, this was a great environment in which to practice stepping outside of myself, and I had the privilege of helping these farmers become their own experts on their unique conflicts and stressors. Acting like I could share their views on planting, fertilizers, machinery, grain elevators, feed lots, veterinary concerns, and inclement weather would be disingenuous as best. Instead, empathetically learning about their world and then creating narratives that aligned with it was a more thoughtful and appealing approach. It required deliberate energy, focus, and discipline, but the rewards, as you'll see, were well worth it.

IMAGERY APPROACH TO CONFLICT MANAGEMENT

DUALISTIC APPROACH TO CONFLICT

ABSTRACT ⟵——— **DUALISM** ———⟶ CONCRETE
ASPECTS OF CONFLICT   ASPECTS OF CONFLICT

UNSCRIPTED		SCRIPTED
Energy • Nuance	**VS.**	Literal • Procedure
Metaphysical • Intuition		Science • Outcomes

Numerous conflict models are based upon a Dualistic Approach. Steer from a **DUALISTIC APPROACH** to an **IMAGERY APPROACH** because the Dualistic Approach limits understanding.

IMAGERY APPROACH: Visual description or figurative language that serves as a representative bridge between the abstract and concrete.

IMAGERY APPROACH TO CONFLICT

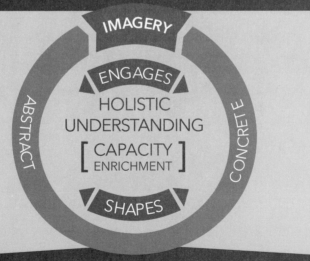

IMAGERY
ENGAGES
HOLISTIC UNDERSTANDING
[CAPACITY
ENRICHMENT]
ABSTRACT
CONCRETE
SHAPES

Conflict Imagery is the buckle that joins the otherwise dualistic abstract and concrete together to engage and shape more holistic understanding. While the two poles might never fully touch, the gap is narrowed and structured in a way that arcs more meaning. This enriched awareness in conflict practitioners can manifest enhanced capacity among disputing parties.

Imagery Touchpoints:

1. If you had to share your biography, what elements of your life would you include? What aspects might you exclude, and why?

2. What examples from your personal experiences with conflict were grayer in nature and did not easily fit into a box of right or wrong or black and white? What was it about these examples that proved to be challenging?

3. What parts of your life already demonstrate an unconscious practice of the Imagery Approach to Conflict Management? If you're unsure whether you've used this approach, where might you start incorporating it?

Imagery Snapshot: *The Imagery Approach to Conflict creates understanding and capacity through a holistic method of bridging the gap between the abstract and the concrete. It's a way of dealing with a dualistic perspective through the union of abstract and concrete realities.*

The Dining Experiment

I recently decided to conduct a secret experiment with participants who were unknowingly part of my mini study. Here is the backdrop. I was invited to a dinner at a nice restaurant. There were five of us ranging from mid-twenties to mid-sixties, with both sexes represented. I felt good about testing my idea on a wide age range of males and females. Additionally, each person held at least a bachelor's degree, and a handful had advanced degrees. Several had lived in states outside of Iowa, and their backgrounds ranged from rural to urban settings. There were those interested in golfing, running, arts, and music in the mix. We had people who were single, dating, divorced, parents, and non-parents in the group. Our faith-based values also varied. In other words, while it was small, it was a mighty and eclectic group.

Here was the experiment. Because we were at a fine-dining establishment with available time and an environment suitable for thoughtful discussions, and because we had a group large enough to provide varied responses but small enough for non-monopolized, meaningful conversation, I decided to see how long it would take for anyone in the group to ask about anyone else present at the table. In other words, I was waiting to see how long it would take for anyone to pose a question like, "How are things going in *your* life?" or, "What's new with *your* work/family/school?" or, "How is *your* hobby treating you?" Picture yourself at a similar dining table. How long do you think it would take most people to ask these types of exploratory questions? Five minutes? Ten minutes? Thirty? An hour?

After dining for nearly two hours, no one had asked these types of discovery questions. I could pretend and say I was shocked, but the fact that I even felt compelled to do the experiment revealed what I had intuited might occur. Don't get me wrong. I'm not shaming this group, nor am I disappointed in them. There were definitely questions asked of each other during the meal, but they were more along the lines of, "What are you ordering?" "How was your meal?" "How far did you run today?" "When are you going golfing again?" Most were close-ended questions, and certainly none were probing enough to learn more about those dining with them. This isn't to say the conversation was superficial. People at the table shared meaningful parts of their lives. Searching for an apartment, starting a new job, and embarking upon a new career were some of the areas explored during the meal. All of this conversation, however, began with people sharing about themselves. The depth of it depended upon what people wanted to discuss about themselves, not what they drew from others.

Why was this happening? Perhaps the people at the table had enough communication skills to share eloquently without the need for people to ask questions about them. Perhaps we were an interesting enough group with ample room to discuss things without anyone needing to probe. Or perhaps our natural bend is to be inwardly focused. It takes more time, attention, and energy to really pay attention to people. This requires a full focus on them and a kind of tempered ego in order to dial into who the people sitting across from you really are. Maybe we're simply too fatigued in our modern age to have what it takes to scratch below the surface and really connect with people. Maybe this is why so many of us spend countless hours dining with our noses in our phones instead of our eyes on the people at the dinner table. Maybe this is why so many are hooked on social media to inform them about the lives of others rather than actually taking a walk with them around a neighborhood park while discussing the wins and pitfalls of the day.

To further unpack my little experiment, several days later, I decided to ask one of the people at the dinner a handful of questions to see if they could answer general questions about me. I've known this person as an acquaintance for four years, and we've known each other in a closer capacity for the past year. As such, I was curious about how he would respond to the following ten questions:

1. What are the names of my three kids?
2. What states have I lived in?
3. What is the name of my consulting business?
4. What, if any, is my political affiliation?
5. What was my last name while I was married?
6. How old am I, or what month was I born in?
7. What, if any, is my religious or denominational membership?
8. What is the first name of my ex-husband?
9. What is my birth order in my family, or how many siblings do I have?
10. Where did I grow up?
11. Bonus question: What's the name of my dog?

One question. Out of these eleven, he could accurately answer only one of them. Six of the questions he could provide partial or relatively accurate answers, but only one answer was fully correct. (Ironically, the question he'd gotten right was my married name prior to my divorce, which happened in a timeframe when he didn't know me). In all fairness to him, when I called, I told him it was for a quick survey, and he didn't need to fret if answers weren't readily coming to mind. I purposely didn't give him any forewarning that I would be calling him with an inquisition.

When I asked the first question about the names of my kids, he paused before responding. Then he said, "This is pretty awful because I should know the names of your kids." I assured him that it wasn't a big deal. He knew the proper name for one and the nickname of another. One child's name slipped his mind entirely, and he didn't know their birth order or ages. A handful of the other questions, he admitted he didn't know at all. I appreciated that he didn't attempt to guess and instead said he couldn't answer the question. It was an enlightening process, and I would encourage similar experiments to learn more about how people create the world around themselves and whether that includes any narratives about the individuals surrounding them. In this particular case, I must not have been center-stage with this person, and I am totally okay with that reality. I don't expect to be the center of his universe. I've been a mom far too long and know the sun and moon don't rise for me alone. Children are some of the best teachers of this lesson.

The goal here is not to pass judgement. Instead, it's to create awareness of how hard we have to work against our natural tendency to be self-focused in many of our thought processes and decision-making.[26] When we become more aware of this, we can improve. Ironically, I also believe most of our self-centered thoughts and decisions are rather superficial. I stated that we need to work against our reflex to be self-focused when it comes to observing and processing our external world, because we have to work against our tendency to merely accept our surface-level self-reflections at face value. In other words, we tend to measure the outside world by our own values and internal constructs. However, these constructs are often what come to mind with little self-resistance, self-editing, or self-observation. After all, it's much easier to go with what easily springs forth. It takes a great deal of effort and assessment to delve into who and what informs those inner workings. Ask any skilled therapist. That's why much of the conversation we have with others is in the neutral, comfortable zone where we discuss what is second nature without really connecting with others on a fundamental level or challenging ourselves to examine who we truly are as individuals. Take a step back and critically assess how you communicate with most people in social settings. Then assess how you communicate with yourself internally during regular, routine days. Many people will find that both of these external and internal communications are rather thin.

We stay in the middle lane. In life, this middle lane works well most of the time. Getting from point A to point B with little resistance or consideration is efficient. This is why highways were designed with these useful middle lanes—they serve the world exceedingly well. However, when experiences in these lanes are unsuccessful, the lanes themselves tend to fail, and a freeway pileup is never good. In the same way, this is why a relationship that appears steady and harmonious might suddenly derail in the throes of conflict. In the blink of an eye, the dynamics of a relationship can suddenly get redefined. Abruptly, the bond is broken by forces we might not even recognize. The other person may feel misunderstood, disrespected, or devalued. We may lack the internal clarity to know ourselves enough to recognize the internal paradigms prompting our perceptions or triggering strong, unexpected reactions. We are driving along on autopilot, and suddenly we approach an expected molehill that has become an unexpected mountain. And the perplexing thing is that often neither party truly understands how or why it, whatever that "it" might be, even happened in the first place. This is why people in disputes who have come to a longstanding impasse often can't even remember the initial origin of the conflict. If strong feelings prevail, the objective facts are no longer relevant, regardless of the trustworthiness of the source or the accuracy of the information. When we fail to truly see, hear, and know others, we overlook that we've steered out of the comfortable middle lane until it's too late. Driving mindlessly with the cruise-control on can be risky business when we don't observe the road signs.

Real engagement with ourselves and others requires creative, deliberate interrogation. We can't approach relationships with the assumption that people will always naturally offer substantive views about themselves. Sometimes it's best to draw people out. Additionally, many individuals spend their whole lives without trying to explore who they truly are. The next time you interact with someone, consider the types of questions you ask them. Are they open questions that seek to elicit meaningful information about them? And the next time you surprise or disturb yourself with your behavior, consider how you process this. Do you pause to ask yourself why? Do you try to connect with your inner self to align internal experience with your external reactions? Initially, these steps might feel inefficient and perhaps even disingenuous. Mastery of any skill requires time, effort, and patience. So start with small aspects of yourself and relationships you're comfortable with. Picture an athlete viewing the practice field versus the game field. Both are important, but an athlete spends far more time and energy on the practice field developing skills to put into play on the game field. Looking at conflict management as a performance-based practice helps create the mindset of skill development. All skill-based endeavors require frequent exercise and conditioning if the goal is peak performance. No musician would sit for a recital without an enormous amount of practice beforehand, no actor would take the stage without rehearsing lines, and no conflict manager should begin formal dispute administration without first honing their craft.

People adept at managing conflict are craftsmen, and most craftsmen develop skills through formal study, following fellow craftsmen they admire and developing their natural abilities. An apprentice learns through a variety of educational experiences. Consider Michelangelo, who by many accounts is the greatest artist of all time. He didn't learn to paint and sculpt through osmosis. While he had an innate talent spotted at an early age, he also spent three years studying at Lorenzo d'Medici's Sculpture Garden and another year with his mentor, Domenico Ghirlandaio. Michelangelo even sought, and received, special permission from the Catholic Church to dissect cadavers at the Monastery of Santo Spirito and the Santa Maria del Santo Spirito convent's hospital in Florence.[27] He knew the best way to paint and sculpt the human body was to see and touch human anatomy from skin to bone. Although frowned upon by the Catholic Church, he spent most of his life dissecting bodies in the pursuit of learning how our outward appearance is determined by all that lies within. By exploring the full human body, he was able to create masterpieces that might not otherwise exist today. Many people get the benefit of touring the Sistine Chapel without realizing the great effort Michelangelo first made to become a master of anatomy. Keep in mind that dealing with a cadaver during this Renaissance period would have been a gruesome task for many. Unpreserved bodies decompose quickly. He and others, like Leonardo da Vinci, firmly believed that an external view of a person did not provide the same insights as looking inside. By understanding the ligaments, bones, muscles, and blood vessels, their art came to life. The external presentation of a man or woman becomes more accurate, more detailed, and more relevant when there is a connection with the internal state. *The Last Judgement* and *The Creation of Adam* are beautiful reminders of his artistic genius that came about through the constant pursuit of excellence by his continual study.

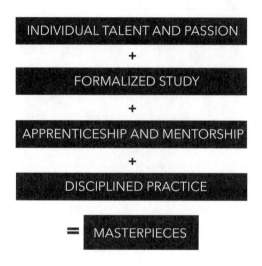

Just as these artists understood the importance of studying the innards of cadavers and the surfaces of living models, thereby holistically embracing all of the human body, we also want many facets of the mundane world to operate the same way. Take your mechanic, for instance. Drivers want them to seamlessly care for the external and internal components of our vehicles. My sweet little Subaru Outback might be cute as all get-out, but I will be severely limited in its use if it fails to drive. It doesn't do much good sitting in the driveway. I need my mechanic to understand the components of my all-terrain SUV inside and out. One doesn't function very well without the other. If I believe my car is only roadworthy when it's built and inspected by those who are authorities on the guts of its systems, why should I lower my standards when it comes to conflict management? I can tell someone all the prescribed steps of the mediation process, and they will have the rote information they need, but putting them into practice is another story. Just like I can be told how to change a car tire, my confidence in dealing with the issue grows exponentially when I actually touch and feel the spare tire while putting the instructions into practice.

The next time you're at a restaurant with friends, try creating your own experiment by observing the types of questions they ask while dining. Or venture out and try experimenting in other environments where questions are a natural part of life. Listen to the questions your mechanic asks when there's car trouble. Think about the inquiries from your doctor if you are ill. How does your hairstylist figure out what you want during a makeover? Then, try your hand at using exploratory questions to see what it feels like to really discover the essence of an individual. Assess whether the types of questions you ask change when you are more mindful about being present with someone. With time, using open-ended, discovery-based questions will become more natural. In the following chapters, we'll explore what to do during the moments when we learn revealing information about others. We'll also spend time figuring out our own internal narratives as they pertain to conflict. We're on the quest to become Michelangelos of conflict management.

Imagery Touchpoints:

1. Create a list of questions you could ask someone at your next social gathering to learn more about them. What types of questions did you create? What types of questions would you want someone to ask you if they were getting to know you better?

2. Think of a hobby or activity that you're passionate about. What steps did you have to take to become skilled at it? What pushed you through the moments when the learning was difficult or frustrating?

3. Consider a movie where the plotline incorporates triumph. What did the characters do to achieve this state? How does this relate to the process of self-awareness and the awareness of others pertaining to the process of conflict management?

Imagery Snapshot: *The practice of discovery-based questions will encourage an outwardly focused perspective on the world rather than our naturally occurring inward focus. Encouraging open dialogue with a mindful attitude produces deeper wisdom.*

Seatbelt Kiley

Personality assessments can be valuable tools that provide a wealth of information. Used properly, they shed light on how people interact with the world around them. (I am an ENTJ for those wedded to Meyers-Briggs, and I am a high D/I for followers of the DiSC Profile.[28] Yes, I'm already aware that I am a very intense soul.) Personality inventories can be great because they reveal natural tendencies and preferences. On the flipside, they aren't always good predictors of how people will respond during specific moments or times of conflict. By simply observing the world around us, we know that not everyone with the same personality profile will respond the same way in a conflict. Five people with the same assessment markers could react very differently during a dispute. Personality alone isn't enough to predict how someone will deal with conflict, and some people deal with it more constructively than others. It's unfortunate that there are certain personality types that get a bad rap and are labeled for how they will deal with conflict because we can find individuals in all realms who are successful conflict managers.

Conversely, having a particular personality type also doesn't automatically guarantee the person is going to be a perfect conflict manager. This is why stereotypes and typecasting can be very counterproductive. For all the doormats and bulldozers out there who have been prematurely pigeonholed, have hope. There's room enough in the china cabinet of life for all of us. As an alleged bulldozer, I am grateful for this perspective. I know bulldozers serve an important purpose, but it can also be confusing when my softer underside doesn't align with the hard shell I'm projecting. It is harmful to label people as "alpha," "lazy," "bitchy," or "spineless" because no one is the sum-total of a single personality trait. In fact, if we use these labels too frequently, we run the risk of living a self-fulfilling prophecy. Words create movement. Give people, and yourself, permission to display the gestalt of personality characteristics that reside within. I promise I'm not always the bull in the china shop, so please invite me to the tea party.

Because our personalities don't chain us to a certain path of success or failure in conflict, we should take heart that one can develop many of the necessary skills, approaches, and philosophies. Life isn't static, and we should have the growth mindset that the more aware we become, the more malleable our personalities can evolve as conflict managers. As previously noted, this is good news for me. If you get to know me, you'll quickly discover that I have a fairly big personality. This is a nice way of saying that people notice my actions and responses—*all* of them. I cheer loudly, I bark loudly, I wail loudly, I laugh loudly, and I move loudly. You get the picture. I do life loudly. This is why any silence from me is concerning for those who know me. They assume that if I'm being quiet something is very wrong because I'm not in performer mode any longer. Let's just say I'm probably not designed to be a professional poker player.

I have a beloved friend and coworker who likes to tease that she gears up and mentally prepares when she sees me entering my "Seatbelt Kiley" moments. She lovingly jokes that when I get amped up, you had better be prepared for a rollercoaster of activity. Put your seatbelt on because Kiley is going to take you for a ride. She once told me that she knows I'm getting ready to work on a big project when I start cleaning the office breakroom. It used to baffle her because she couldn't figure out why I was spending my time cleaning when there were important functions to focus on. Then she realized it was like my energy needed to find an outlet before beginning a big mental task, so I engage in the menial duty of cleaning the heck out of a workspace before embarking upon the critical mission. What can I say? Seatbelt Kiley does what she's gotta do.

So what does Seatbelt Kiley have to do with conflict management? Well, it offers the assurance that you are multifaceted. It isn't just one aspect of your personality that always shows up, and that's certainly never the case when dealing with conflict. Furthermore, when the unflattering aspects of yourself come out to play, allowing yourself some grace is a much wiser approach than shaming yourself. Take a pause instead and re-assess.

I've described my large personality as my potential pitfall, but for you, it may be a habit of allowing yourself to be railroaded when you wish to voice yourself and be seen. It may be outwardly presenting yourself as lazy when what you really feel inside is confusion. Or it might be a reversion to emotional instability when you desire harmony. Whatever externally manifests for you is okay. Who you are is just fine. Who you are is more than enough. Meet yourself where you are and start to study yourself with an open, mindful approach. Once we start doing this, then we can start determining what it is within ourselves that expresses itself externally. When we start making connections between our internal state and our external presentation, we can start embracing the unique imagery that speaks to the essence of who we really are. This imagery creates illustrations and imaginative power that both service our conflict management skills. Then, when those skills are honed, we can use this imagery, illustration, and imagination to help others manage their conflicts. When we have dealt with our own essence, we can then focus on others to help them discover their authentic selves. Our essence is more profound than any personality assessment can measure.

Tapping into our personal essence, core, and spirit is often a challenging process because there are no hard and fast rules about how to go about it. While interviewing participants for my dissertation study, I realized a common thread among them—these people were adept at mediation because they knew themselves. They didn't try to fashion themselves into something else or push a conflict management style that didn't fit well with them. When I probed further, however, they didn't specifically articulate their internal compass. Instead, they offered up imagery statements that shed light on their inner being and convictions. Remember, they provided examples tied to art, music, gardening, theater, sports, engineering, technology, fashion, etc., to verbalize their conflict management and mediation skills rooted in abstract philosophies. These illustrations helped them conceptualize those abstract philosophies in the concrete, in tangibles. Though none were asked to use imagery or imagination to help me understand their mediation careers, every single person put it to good use.

Let's return to my dining experiment and follow-up conversation where I asked one of the diners to answer ten questions about me. The person who could only answer one question accurately wasn't a seasoned mediator, so I decided to continue the experiment with two coworkers, asking them the same questions. One mediator has known me for two years and has been mediating for the same period of time. He could accurately answer six of the ten questions. The other mediator has known me for six years and has been mediating for more than thirty. She could answer all off them, plus the bonus question about my dog. She missed one state where I had lived, Missouri, but considering I had only lived there for less than a year, this was really quite impressive.

Because this mini experiment wasn't conducted using controlled methodologies, there is no scientific way of knowing whether she could more readily answer questions because she has known me longer or because of her age, gender, or upbringing. However, it's safe to say that her ability as a conflict management practitioner has served her well. She focused on who I am and learned about me during our interactions together. Having witnessed her in mediation sessions, as a trainer, and in other personal and professional settings, I strongly believe this to be true. She has a profound and gifted ability to see—I mean *really* see—people, and she quickly connects with them at a deep level. She intuitively knows when and how to outwardly focus on them to dial into their core personality, using her internal compass to guide her. Once she discovers their natural bend, she then takes who she is and finds common ground with that individual based on what resonates with them specifically. This isn't to say that she dishonors her own fundamentals. Rather, she uses the fundamentals within herself to speak to the fundamentals in others. It's pretty amazing to witness. She's also the person who gave me the moniker of "Seatbelt Kiley." That image is still in use today because people connect with the idea of a seatbelt and my temperament. In Iowa, a far-flung, rural state, it's difficult for Iowans to navigate the state and keep gainful employment without the ability to drive, and public transportation isn't widely used or available, so almost every adult drives themselves. So in Iowa, her illustration of Seatbelt Kiley makes sense to most of the people around her. Brilliant, eh? Without being told to do so, she knew to present an image about my internal state using an external example that holds meaning to her audience. If we were in a city or country where self-driving isn't prevalent, this example might not hold as much value. But I guarantee she would provide a different image to help them gain clarity about me. Maybe she would nickname me "Rollercoaster Kiley" or "Speedboat Kiley" depending on the audience. Regardless of the title, it conveys that spending time with me can be intense. A wild ride, indeed.

If we are trying to help illustrate a concept to a person, should the illustration be geared strictly to them or strictly to ourselves? Well, neither. A non-dual approach with an artful mix of both is most prudent. Either/or isn't helpful in these situations. I won't likely be able to create an accurate or meaningful illustration for others if I don't also integrate myself with the image. People can feel when something grows from a place of authentic, genuine intent. This is why a handful of mediators can often assess the same conflict scenario and dial into different components of the situation. They will ask different questions and focus on different parts of the conflict and personalities involved. However, they'll come to a consensus that holds value for all parties. Differences within the process stem from the mediators using their own internal compasses to guide themselves toward messages that speak directly to the parties. This is more of an art than a science, which is why the prescriptive steps taught in most mediation and conflict management manuals only cover a small part of what makes conflict resolution achievable.

I discovered firsthand the complexity of joining differing worlds when I was asked by Iowa Farm Bureau to present to its members. Farm Bureau is an insurance and lobbying group representing the agri-culture industry, and it has a large membership in Iowa. I was eager to accept this invitation as I really enjoy speaking to individuals from all walks of life and frequently provide presentations, facilitations, and consultations to people and organizations across the country. However, I typically speak to learners who are seeking to impart the knowledge and curriculum into their own professions. For example, I often conduct train-the-trainer sessions or tailor the teachings to professionals in their respective fields. This time, I was asked to work directly with the whole family, not just the operator or active farmer. Instead of speaking to the farm insurance agent, banker, attorney, or accountant as is customary, the goal of the program was to help these families cope with the unique attributes associated with farm stress. I was excited to embrace this challenge and come up with something that hopefully would educate and empower them to deal with the realities of farm stress. What resulted is a platform now coined "The Stress Personality Tool Types." This tool will be explored in greater detail in the next chapter so you can see how I attempted to connect the need to create symbols these farm families could relate to with the need to be authentic to my urban background. Stay tuned to see how Farmer and City Slicker unite.

Imagery Touchpoints:

1. If you have completed any personality inventories, what aspects did you enjoy or dislike? What parts were accurate or confusing to you? How might these indicators shed light on how you deal with conflict? If you haven't done a personality inventory, consider participating in one so you can gain insights into the experience.

2. I was described as "Seatbelt Kiley" in this chapter. How might someone describe you if they were asked to give you a moniker? What would this title convey? Why does it make you feel comfortable or uncomfortable?

3. When I was asked to present to farmers, I had to take a step back to connect their worldview with mine. Think of a time when you had to link up with a person, group, or entity outside of your paradigm. How did you deal with it? What aspects of this process were successful or unsuccessful from your vantage point?

Imagery Snapshot: *People are complex, multi-faceted creatures, and our dominant traits are only some expressions of who we are underneath. The capacity to develop and grow beyond our natural state can be nurtured.*

Farm and City

When Farm Bureau asked me to work with farm families dealing with stress, I was extremely excited to work with this group. After all, agriculture is the backbone of our nation and certainly the state of Iowa. At the time of this writing, nearly 90 percent of the state's land is farmed, and there are over 88,600 farmsteads in the state.[29] The land is used for crop and livestock production, and the state ranks number one in the nation for the production of soybeans, corn, pork, and eggs. Iowa also leads the United States in the production of ethanol and biodiesel. The corn commodity alone generates nearly $10 billion for the state: $10,000,000,000! This astonishing number is just for one crop, and Iowa produces many other important crops. Farming in Iowa is no small business; it's a tough one where only the strong survive. It's no wonder that it's a stressful enterprise.

Farming is so stressful, in fact, that the US Centers for Disease Control and Prevention has flagged the industry due to its markedly high suicide rates.[30] In fact, the CDC indicates that the farming, fishing, and forestry professions have some of the highest suicide rates in the nation across all careers. Without getting into the metaphorical weeds of farming, here is the fundamental reason why it's so stressful: very little of the farming world is within the control of the farmer. Fluctuating crop and livestock prices, variable input expenses, the weather, health insurance availability and costs, interest rates on loans, rent prices, equipment costs, and upkeep are just some of the areas that today's farmer has to contend with, and these things don't go away. Farmers face these issues every season. Therefore, it stands to reason that the one constant in the world of a farmer is change. In addition, the complexity of farming and the costs involved have required many farmers and their spouses to keep off-farm employment to sustain their standards of living. For instance, some work outside the farm for the access to affordable healthcare. It's a complicated endeavor to keep the modern farm viable.

What makes farming unique compared to many other professions is that this business is often a family affair, and the tasks don't end when the clock strikes five. These people live and breathe their business. When most of us end our workday, we get to shift into our home life. For the farmer, their homestead often also serves as their accounting office, restaurant, daycare center, repair shop, entertainment venue, manufacturing headquarters, and management site. Few other business models meld home and work so closely that even the family members themselves often don't know where one begins and one ends. So when times get tough, it's very hard, if not impossible, to compartmentalize the functions of the business and the home. And if you're a livestock producer, you likely don't have the luxury of going on a vacation to get a reprieve because animals need to be tended to daily. It's cost-prohibitive to hire people to care for livestock if the markets aren't doing well and money is tight. So the stress mounts with few available outlets.

Thankfully, organizations like Farm Bureau are responding to the need for behavioral and mental health interventions. Hopefully

American culture is becoming wiser at identifying and appreciating the very real stress that farmers and their families face. And it's not just stressful for the farmer but the family unit as well. After all, think about the multifaceted roles that many farm family members assume. A wife might have an off-farm job to provide a steady salary and benefits and still serve as the bookkeeper, manager, and errand-runner for the farm operations. Meanwhile, she is also tending to the needs of the home and the children of the household. It's a complicated, and sometimes intense, existence. Yet, the idea of selling the farm and venturing into another occupation is a rare occurrence in this state. Farmers are wedded to the legacy of the land. Selling their piece of ground is considered a deep failure of both business and family. Imagine living with that pressure, day in and day out, season upon season. It's no wonder stress is high for farmers, and because of the rural nature of farming, there is a woefully inadequate availability of good mental health resources.

Seeing the need, Farm Bureau decided to reach out in search of a brief training program that could be put together for farmers and their family members, and they asked that the curriculum specifically address how to cope with farm stress. I thought about this for some time before deciding the proper course of action. It was feasible to simply list the variables that create stress in the lives of farmers, but this approach wouldn't bring anything new to light, and I certainly wouldn't be sharing anything they didn't already experience on a regular basis. Plus, how could a city gal like myself be credible with this group if I talked about stress through sterile statistics about rural Iowa that I had studied from the safety of an urban office chair? It would be disingenuous at best. I could feel the growing disconnect as I visualized myself speaking to the group. They would be too polite to roll their eyes, but I could almost guarantee lots of mental eye rolls.

The thing I had going for me is that I have spent ten years

working with other family industries in my training, consulting, and mediation work. The key was to find common ground. I began reflecting on what I had learned from farmers and professionals who work with them. Farmers are very hands-on people who hold dear the keenly strong value of family legacy and stewardship. Preservation of the homestead is extremely important. This could serve as the common denominator among us. I, too, value family and show this through my DIY efforts to make sure my home is a creative, eclectic, and comfortable environment for my three kids. Nothing gives me more joy than giving something in my home new life so my kids and I can cherish it together. My technical carpentry skills aren't superior, but I have enough knowledge to use a toolbox with a degree of aptitude. I've also overseen several larger home remodeling projects. This is where I imagined I could make a connection with these farm families—matters of the homestead and renovation.

The literal visualization of a homestead remodeling project served as the framework to teach about stress management in a meaningful way. Many farm homesteads are quite old, so updates are a natural part of this type of home ownership. As a result, the training session began by asking them to picture their kitchen needing an update, as everyone in the family would appreciate a functional cooking space. The primary goal of this renovation project was to get more light into the kitchen, so the very old windows needed to be replaced. They were asked to visualize their toolbox and share the top ten tools they might need for the project. Then they were asked why they included those tools and whether one tool was more valuable to them than another. Collectively, everyone agreed that each tool served a different purpose and excluding any of these tools would make a building project more difficult. I then stated that each one of us is like a tool with a use it is designed to perform best. We then pictured the uses of five tools—a tape measure, a level, a hammer, pliers, and a screwdriver. I explained that we have a natural tendency to be like one of these five metaphorical tools when dealing with stress, and we conducted the following exercise to reveal the primary "stress tool" type an individual might utilize.

A helpful way to determine your personal response to stress and the tools you use is to consider the following when you experience extreme stress. Do you…

1. become more passive or more active in behaviors?

2. become more introverted or more extroverted with communication?

3. become more cooperative or more competitive with others?

4. become more analytical or more impulsive with decision-making?

5. become more avoidant or more engaging with the problem?

Using this feedback, place yourself into one of the tool categories using these guidelines:

Tape Measure

During stress, the Tape Measure is seen as the "Evaluator."
How they primarily function: Calculate and Gauge
What they value: Accuracy, Details, Facts, Plans, Logic
What they need: Information
Environments they thrive in: Rules, Standards, Timeframes, Agendas, Instructions, Systems
How others struggle with this temperament: Rigidity, Emotional unavailability, Fixation
Communication they do not need: Face-to-face [Instead: Technology-based]
Areas for personal growth: Flexibility, Emotional openness, Compromise
Concerns for this type: Paralyzed by their need for perfection

Level

During stress, the Level is seen as the "Zen".
How they primarily function: Balance and Align
What they value: Peace, Stillness, Order, Evenness, Pauses
What they need: Calm
Environments they thrive in: Relaxed, Space, Harmony, Smooth processes, Time, Traditions
How others struggle with this temperament: Avoidant, Paralysis, Apathy
Communication they do not need: Multiple interactions [Instead: Breaks between]
Areas for personal growth: Sense of urgency, Appreciating extremes, Opposing views
Concerns for this type: Internalize their worries when they should vocalize

Pliers

During stress, the Pliers are seen as the "Mediator".
How they primarily function: Grasp and Bend
What they value: Negotiation, Flexibility, Compromise, Understanding, Essence
What they need: Meaning
Environments they thrive in: Philosophy, Communication, Interventions, Emotions, Complex strategies, Forecasting
How others struggle with this temperament: Personal veil, Vague, Transaction-averse
Communication they do not need: Technology-based [Instead: Face-to-face]
Areas for personal growth: Individual identity, Boundaries, Conciseness
Concerns for this type: Their identity is confusing for others to pinpoint

Screwdriver

During stress, the Screwdriver is seen as the "Networker".
How they primarily function: Intertwine and Fasten
What they value: Interactions, Synergy, Teamwork, Conciliation, Union
What they need: Connection
Environments they thrive in: People-pleasing, Events, Meetings, Consulting, Brainstorming, Facilitation
How others struggle with this temperament: Busyness, Dependency, Smothering
Communication they do not need: Sporadic exchanges [Instead: Regular contact]
Areas for personal growth: Silence, Individuality, Space
Concerns for this type: Creating their personal boundaries

Hammer

During stress, the Hammer is seen as the "Competitor".
How they primarily function: Drive and Deconstruct
What they value: Strength, Energy, Impact, Tangibles, Power
What they need: Outcomes
Environments they thrive in: Movement, Passion, Major tasks, Visuals, End goals, Broad plans
How others struggle with this temperament: Monopolize, Harshness, Disruption
Communication they do not need: Indirect messages [Instead: Clear statements]
Areas for personal growth: Nuance, Appreciating pauses, Gentleness
Concerns for this type: Guilt after they become explosive with others

The following table is a side-by-side comparison to help create personal awareness and evaluate the temperaments of those around you:

	TAPE MEASURE	LEVEL
During stress, they are seen as the...	*Evaluator*	*Zen*
How they primarily function	Calculate and Gauge	Balance and Align
What they value	Accuracy, Details, Facts, Plans, Logic	Peace, Stillness, Order, Evenness, Pauses
What they need	Information	Calm
Environments they thrive in	Rules, Standards, Timeframes, Agendas, Instructions, Systems	Relaxed, Space, Harmony, Smooth processes, Time, Traditions
Struggles others have with this temperament	Rigidity, Emotional unavailability, Fixation	Avoidant, Paralysis, Apathy
Communication they do not prefer	Face-to-face [Instead: Technology-based]	Multiple interactions [Instead: Breaks between]
Areas for their personal growth	Flexibility, Emotional openness, Compromise	Sense of urgency, Appreciating extremes, Opposing views
Concerns for this type	Paralyzed by their need for perfection	Internalize and do not vocalize their worries

HAMMER	PLIERS	SCREWDRIVER
Competitor	*Mediator*	*Networker*
Drive and Deconstruct	Grasp and Bend	Intertwine and Fasten
Strength, Energy, Impact, Tangibles, Power	Negotiation, Flexibility, Compromise, Understanding, Essence	Interactions, Synergy, Teamwork, Conciliation, Union
Outcomes	Meaning	Connection
Movement, Passion, Major tasks, Visuals, End goals, Broad plans	Philosophy, Communication, Interventions, Emotions, Complex strategies, Forecasting	People-pleasing, Events, Meetings, Consulting, Brain-storming, Facilitation
Monopolize, Harshness, Disruption	Personal veil, Vague, Transac-tion-adverse	Busyness, Dependency, Smothering
Indirect messages [Instead: Clear statements]	Technology-based [Instead: Face-to-face]	Sporadic exchanges [Instead: Regular contact]
Nuance, Appreciating pauses, Gentleness	Individual identity, Boundaries, Conciseness	Silence, Individuality, Space
Guilt after they become explosive with others	Their identity is confusing for others to pinpoint	Creating their personal boundaries

After identifying their stress tool types, we continued the metaphor of installing the kitchen window with and without the five tools. Scenarios were played out that might occur during the remodeling process, including each step that might benefit best from one of the individual tools. The participants were reminded that everyone has the ability to utilize any of the tools when dealing with stress. But we tend to grab our preferred tool because it's what we set at the top of our tool bag—it's natural to use what's most available. During stress that involves conflict, consider the tools that others naturally reach for, and use this knowledge to work together to constructively design, change, or remove the stress. Try not to assume that others know your needs or your stress-management preferences. Additionally, remember that all tools have value and purpose. During times of stress tied to conflict, appreciate that the approaches you use aren't in competition with those of others. Stress becomes easier to manage when expectations and acceptance are in place.

Once the group processed the kitchen remodeling scenario, we closed the training session with the analogy of the window and the importance of shedding light on areas that serve a purpose in our lives. Literally, the kitchen needs more light to become a better functioning space; metaphorically, conflict requires illumination to produce solutions.

As the training wrapped up, I took a deep breath, preparing myself to determine whether it had hit the mark. I mustered up the confidence to ask the farm family members if they had any comments on the session. Since this was a pilot training session, we were in uncharted territory.

A gentlemen piped up and said, "My family is made up entirely of hammers. What do we do when all of our toolboxes are filled with the same tool, especially when they're all hammers? Doesn't that make us a tough group?"

He never spoke using the psychobabble commonly associated with personality assessments, stress management, and conflict resolution materials. Instead, he spoke in very direct terms about the hammer. He had gotten the gist of the message. A wonderful conversation unfolded, and I am confident that's because we were engaging our imaginations in a dialogue using imagery and illustrations that they valued and I understood. We were speaking the same, shared language. Afterward, a family member sent an email and asked how she might determine the tools used by other members of the family that hadn't attended the training. Upon receiving this email, it was evident we had struck training gold!

I didn't do anything magical in the session; all I'd done was make sure the family members felt genuinely seen. I also made sure they could see me. We found a common thread to bring everyone together. The imagery, illustrations, and imagination required to really internalize the training materials resonated both with me as the teacher and them as the learners. When we put the concept of farm stress and conflict management into terms related to a simple toolbox, common tools, and a regular home remodel, we created a synergy. Young, old, male, female, parent, child, owner, operator—everyone understood the foundation of the conversation. And as a self-admitted Hammer during stress and conflict, I was pumped to so quickly witness tangible results from our new training method.

As an individual who appreciates visual learning tools, I offered a simple handout for the participants to take with them into their daily lives. It provides a basic framework that ties together the verbal and visual aspects of a complex topic using various images, illustrations, and imagination to connect the abstract with the concrete. It's less threatening and confusing when the tangible is brought to life in practical ways. Set pomp, bravado, and academia aside. Instead, communicate, teach, and clarify with humility. After all, a hammer doesn't have to destroy the nail to hold the windowsill together.

Using the Tools

People respond to stress differently depending on their stress-tolerance ability and their general temperament. The variables that trigger stress are specific to each person because individuals experience and process the world around them uniquely.

Everyone has the ability to use all of the tools in the tool box, though we likely have a preferred tool we rely on under pressure. Consider which tool you gravitate toward during stress or conflict, and observe which tools others around you use. Knowledge of both will increase constructive problem-solving and decrease burdens related to stress. With realistic expectations and acceptance, issues become easier to manage.

All tools have value and purpose. Try to see your approach and those of others as not being in competition with each other. Each has its own meaningful design to contribute.

What can you learn from your tool type and that of those around you?

Use this imagery and awareness to improve self-recognition, relationships, efficiencies, coping skills, and goal achievement.

Imagery Touchpoints:

1. Complete the Stress Personality Tool Types inventory. Picture yourself installing a kitchen window and recognizing the value of your preferred tool type. Picture the preferred tool types found within your own family. How might this information help you when dealing with interfamily conflict?

2. Do you interact with people who have vastly different functions in life than yourself—perhaps a technology professional, a nurse, a mechanic, a graphic designer? What images and illustrations come to mind that you might connect to so that constructive imagination can unfold?

3. Think of a television show or a movie that used a tangible visual or verbal aid to convey a complex message. What was it, and how did it reveal the abstract message? For example, in the movie *Cast Away*, Tom Hanks becomes best friends with a volleyball he names Wilson to illustrate the need for companionship and intimacy. When Wilson gets lost, his tears aren't for the volleyball. While the movie never states it outright, the tears are for the loss of friendship and the innate human need to belong to community.

Imagery Snapshot: *When dealing with a group, it is as important (maybe even more so) to understand how personalities interact as it is to be aware of how your own personality impacts others. Watch for the subtle and overt cues people provide about their temperaments.*

Conflict Software Development

Let me be the first to say that technology and I are not friends. I revealed earlier that instruction manuals and traffic jams elicit tantrums; technology has the power to do the same. Nothing will flip an otherwise good day on its head like a technology issue. I've come close to chucking my cell phone and laptop across the room more than I care to admit. Classy, Kiley.

Why, then, should we use the illustration of hardware and software to demonstrate how to shift into the identification of our conflict imagery? Because I try in earnest to practice what I preach. If you're being told to externally focus on the elements that define others, I need to do the same. Lots of people find technology to be quite rewarding. The field of technology is a livelihood for many people. So this chapter is a tribute to the tech-savvy gurus I adore for continually making the world an easier place in which to operate. My hat goes off to you!

I'm told software and hardware are important components of

technology, and my watered-down definition of the difference between the two is this: the hardware is the physical apparatus and the software is the programming, the interface between the operator and the piece of equipment.[31] In other words, that trusty old laptop I want to hurl across the room needs software to keep it functioning. Apparently, screaming profanities at the device doesn't do much to change its operational power.

In this analogy, as the conflict manager, you are the operator, the hardware is the Imagery Approach to Conflict Management, and the software is the information and background unique to you. You develop the interface between you as the practitioner and your conflict management skill set through a holistic understanding about what created you. From the moment we take our first breath, we are being molded into who we are. Essentially, it's the butterfly effect in action. In our lives, the tiniest movements create massive change, and we are not stagnant beings.

In my dissertation study, it quickly became evident that many of our lived experiences shape our personal lens on conflict. It was also clear that no universal experience could guarantee mediator success. Rather, it appeared that interpretation was the key to how an experience impacted them. For instance, two mediators in the study were childhood immigrants. Their perspectives on the experience of immigration, however, were quite different. One person indicated that the anxiety of living in a foreign country meant helicopter parenting, with their mom and dad constantly concerned about loosening the reins. The other person indicated that their immigrant parents were so busy working that it allowed a huge degree of freedom to explore the world.

Despite these differences, both mediators described their immigration experiences when discussing their backgrounds and the role the experiences might play in their conflict management styles.

Another individual referenced being raised by parents of two different nationalities and its cultural impact. Several people described getting divorced, though their viewpoints varied widely. Interestingly, one person wished their parents had divorced since their childhood was tumultuous. Others described raising children and how that affects their conflict management approach. There were people highly impacted by religious upbringings, families involved in foster care, living in poverty, continually changing homes and school situations, and being reared by overtly strict parents. Political affiliations were also mentioned, along with education and the influence of key adults in their childhood. Commitment to volunteerism, social justice, and academic excellence were also cited as influential factors growing up. Some embraced their upbringing and their past while others had rebelled. Each of the mediators had aspects of their background that cued their approach to conflict management.

Interestingly, I later learned that some people were divorced but hadn't discussed it in the interview. Others had issues surrounding childhood poverty who chose not to elaborate. It was becoming clear that there is no general formula about what impacts views on conflict, or how. What we *can* generalize is this: consciously or not, what people carry within themselves becomes the essence of their scripts used to create worldviews and perceptions. The energy, power, and definitions they give these scripts is the method by which they create imagery regarding their beliefs, perspectives, and approaches to conflict. In other words, it's not enough to say, "Childhood poverty impacts views on conflict." This is why we should avoid statements in broad brushstrokes. There are too many outside factors and the interplay among countless other variables is unique to an individual. It's the dynamism that counts, whether it's positive or negative, weak or strong, quick or extended.

The key to imagery development is the awareness of triggers, situations, events, and factors that influence you as an individual. They are yours alone to own. This is why we can witness unique imaginations among members of the same family, even between identical twins. The individual messages we ascribe to the most impactful experiences of our lives drive our imaginations. Only you can decide what variables are important to you and why. And it doesn't have to be stereotypically positive or negative for it to matter. From this starting point, our imagination becomes the tool used to create the metaphors, images, and depictions we provide to the outside world to describe our internal state.

The process of identifying inner scripts can feel like a daunting task if self-discovery is unfamiliar to you. What can be helpful is to map out our internal markers. Much like the explorers Lewis and Clark, the process of any kind of map-making requires a particular combination of attention to detail and broad observation. Amazingly, Lewis and Clark created 140 maps from their trail experiences with their slave, York. And interestingly, they produced these maps by establishing latitude and longitude through their celestial observations.[32] One could assume that if the goal is to map a foot trail, the cartographers would be paying attention to the ground below them. Instead, they used the sky to provide information and enlighten them about the land they surveyed. It's an ancient technique that has proven to be highly accurate even by today's technological standards. Comparisons of modern satellite maps to early hand-drawn maps show remarkable similarities. The use of cosmic, aerial evidence, namely the stars, helped guide their feet so they could ultimately map these experiences. In the same way, we need to grab our emotional telescopes when we study how our perspectives on our external experiences align with our internal states to inform what I am calling our Personal Conflict Management Imagery Framework.

We can identify this framework through the process of charting the imagery we associate with conflict. The following is a set of exercises you can use to discover the perspectives you hold on conflict and what aspects of your background have shaped this narrative. It's important to complete these exercises in the spirit of transparency, affirmation, and non-judgement. There is no right or wrong about what has shaped your views. The goal is to simply unearth and explore what impacts you so we can eventually plot your unique Personal Conflict Management Imagery Framework, which you'll tap into when managing conflict. The process alone of identifying these markers can have a powerful ability to show us why we associate certain things with conflict, and why these views might vary greatly from those around us. This mindful approach can be a useful tool to create self-awareness and empathy. This guided methodology allows us to better articulate our internal state and beliefs about conflict to ourselves and others through the imagery of the external. If we choose, we can share this imagery framework with others, or we can simply decide to let the information help us become better practitioners of conflict management.

You might need to take some time to complete the following steps, and they may need to be revisited over time as our level of awareness evolves or life circumstances change. This exploration should be viewed as iterative in nature because our lives and personalities are dynamic, not cemented. Progress, not perfection, is the aim when embracing our authentic inner selves. Once we begin doing this, we then require less acceptance from others about our external manifestations.

Carve out the space, resources, and time you need to mindfully complete these exercises, so when we rejoin in the next chapter, we can discuss how to put the Personal Conflict Imagery Framework into action. This is where the rubber meets the road.

Imagery Touchpoints:

1. Complete the Conflict Imagery Charting exercise below. How does the process of going through this exercise help you better understand the behaviors, decisions, and external manifestations you see from others?

2. Think about people in your life who are close to you and reflect on the lived experiences they might decide to integrate as conflict-shaping markers in their lives.

3. Identify a famous peacekeeper and a famous combatant. Pretend you are their public relations manager tasked with writing a headline for a magazine that expresses their outlooks on conflict. How would you write this headline and ensure its accuracy?

Imagery Snapshot: *Plotting and charting our imagery manifestations is an ongoing process because our internal state evolves over time through awareness and experience. It's important to recognize that this is the same for others as well.*

CONFLICT IMAGERY CHARTING

These exercises will help you navigate your perspective on conflict, with the end goal of creating the imagery you tie to conflict. This imagery will guide your conflict management style or approach.

1. What are the initial thoughts, feelings, or memories you associate with conflict?

_____

_____

_____

_____

_____

_____

_____

_____

_____

_____

_____

_____

_____

_____

_____

_____

2. Circle the top five emotions you connect with conflict.

anger	discomfort	love	hurt
sadness	depression	fear	relief
anxiety	acceptance	avoidance	tension
happiness	enjoyment	gloom	loneliness
compassion	peace	irritation	gladness

horror	desperation	terror	bitterness
loss	hopelessness	grief	amusement
trouble	contentment	mourning	confusion
stress	excitement	pride	joy
worry	heartbreak	panic	satisfaction
nervousness	misery	connection	loathing
revulsion	dislike	disturbance	calm
aversion	offense	serenity	withdrawal
resignation	acceptance	control	disapproval
disturbed	annoyance	frustration	patience
insult	still	cheated	composed
challenged	stunned	pleasure	doubt
delight	vengeance	contrary	disappointment
fury	anticipation	peeved	eagerness
interest	unhappiness		

3. What do you think contributes to the emotions you hold about conflict?

_____

_____

_____

_____

_____

_____

_____

_____

_____

_____

_____

_____

_____

_____

4. Reflect upon your background and identify specific events, circumstances, or influences related to the following:

Notable personal history: _____

_____

_____

Prior professional experience:_____

_____

_____

Formal education: _____

_____

_____

Mediation preference: _____

_____

_____

Family dynamics: _____

_____

_____

Personal values: _____

_____

_____

5. Consider the interests, hobbies, memories, or communities you are very familiar with and/or enjoy. The following are themes to help facilitate your thinking:

Outdoors (e.g. Hiking):_____

Music (e.g. The Beatles):_____

Travel (e.g. Beaches): _____

Theatre (e.g. Broadway play):_____

Architecture (e.g. Victorian):_____

Art (e.g. Picasso):_____

Games (e.g. Poker):_____

Food (e.g. Steak): _____

Medicine (e.g. Heart attack):_____

Weddings (e.g. Honeymoon): _____

School (e.g. Playground):_____

Sports (e.g. Football):_____

Animals (e.g. Dogs):_____

Dance (e.g. Ballroom):_____

Technology (e.g. PlayStation):_____

Clothing (e.g. Purses):_____

Real-estate (e.g. Renovations):_____

Dating (e.g. E-Harmony):_____

Other: _____

Other: _____

Now you are going to link these five steps together to create your Personal Conflict Imagery Framework, which can be a written statement or visual picture.

Example:
1. I engage in conflict and find it useful for change.
2. I believe this because my parents divorced and then later successfully remarried.
3. I used to be a teacher, so I am comfortable with people of all ages, abilities, and temperaments.
4. I traveled a lot with family...

CONFLICT IMAGERY: Conflict is like traveling by plane. You have a destination in mind, so you spend time packing, going through security, and waiting in line, which is necessary to get to your intended location. Along the way, you see different kinds of travelers, and you might feel overwhelmed and tired, but eventually you arrive safely.

YOUR PERSONAL CONFLICT IMAGERY FRAMEWORK

[STATEMENT/PICTURE]: (Write or Sketch below)

Puzzle Pieces and Photographs

There are many ways to approach a jigsaw puzzle, but most would agree the pieces should first face up. It's possible to put a puzzle together with pieces facing down, but that isn't the easiest method, nor does it reveal a picture upon completion. Once the pieces are upright, every method begins with the decision about where to start. You can begin with the edges or start in the middle and work outward, or you can group similar pieces according to detail, image, or color.

Joining conflict and imagery is like assembling an intricate 10,000-piece puzzle designed specifically for you. No two identical puzzles exist, so the creation process is going to be different for each individual. While there are five different sections of the Conflict Image Charting Model, the discovery process doesn't have to follow a linear order. If a section resonates more, feels easier to complete, or seems more naturally fitting, then work on that section first. Just like doing a puzzle, it's important to have a broad workspace to be effective. A puzzle isn't easily assembled if the workspace is the same size or smaller than the completed puzzle. Nor is it wise to try to assemble a puzzle on a table used for other tasks, too, because rarely is a complicated puzzle completed in one sitting. The same goes for the conflict management and imagery discovery process. Start very broadly and understand that the process will be ongoing. If an area stalls or feels stuck, switch to a new area with a fresh perspective. Sometimes the alignment of the nooks and knobs of two compatible puzzle pieces will jump out just by taking a break or working on a new area.

As you go through the Conflict Imagery Charting Model, think about the aspects that relate to your experiences and beliefs about conflict that aren't necessarily negative or related to traditional ideas of disputes. In many cultures, conflict is instantly associated with adversity and punishment. However, it's healthier to embrace the notion that conflict is really just the state of two things appearing to be in opposition or competition with one another. For instance, high versus low can be in conflict, but why? Those who surf know that the ocean has both a high tide and low tide. It's as objective as that. Furthermore, the ocean's state cannot simultaneously be at high and low tide. However, both are necessary at different times. One isn't inherently good or bad, and one isn't inherently better or worse than the other. No surfer would ever want a world where only high tide or low tide existed. Both are necessary to clean the water, circulate nutrition, and create renewable energy. High and low both serving their natural purpose. Opposition and competition are not necessarily negative.

For this reason, it's important to consider all the circumstances, education, upbringing, traditions, and experiences that shape our internal constructs about conflict. Focusing on just the negative, challenging, and difficult aspects of conflict creates a dualistic environment in which a holistic perspective will not flourish. For example, some families rarely "fight" out loud, yet they might have more toxic relationships than in a family who confronts the issues at hand loudly and then moves on without harboring resentments. There are individuals who pepper language with expletives and have more compassion for others than those who politely communicate their words. This is not to advocate yelling, cursing, or intense dialogue, but some people constructively use unconventional ways of interaction. The point is to think about everything—past and present, positive and negative—that collectively impacts your conflict worldview with an open, mindful, and non-judgmental perspective to ensure you aren't disregarding components because you're worried they might be unacceptable. Consider the common phenomenon of divorce. Some people have bitter divorces, while others divorce more amicably. I have a dear friend who has become good friends with her ex-husband's girlfriend. It might not be traditional, but good for them for figuring out how to chart that universe.

As you consider your history, reflect on anything and everything that might be influential. Start broadly. The mediators from the study had a wide range of life experience that impacted their conflict management styles. Going into the research, being an immigrant is not necessarily the first thing that would come to my mind about mediation and conflict styles. Nonetheless it was brought up more than once as an influential variable. Non-profit experience, volunteering opportunities, foster care exchanges, career endeavors, adoption scenarios, traveling, pet ownership, financial security, and family dynamics are just a few other examples that were brought to light during the research process. If you are struggling to get started, here are few concepts to ponder:

Identifying Your Biographical Conflict Narratives

1. Give an example of a strongly positive or negative classroom experience you had.

2. Think of your childhood neighborhood exchanges.

3. Contemplate religious touchpoints that influence you.

4. Describe any atypical or impactful travel or living experiences you've had.

5. Consider any major medical issues or emergencies in your life.

6. Review your formal education for the philosophies and theories you learned.

7. Reflect upon activities or hobbies that resonate with you.

8. Ponder the family interactions surrounding you.

9. Assess how you give and receive feedback in structured versus informal environments.

10. Identify positive or negative security or resource topics (food, housing, fitness, finance, clothing).

11. Inventory friendships and mentorships.

12. Think about your career inspirations.

13. Consider the geographic and demographic influences in your life.

14. Ponder the type of music, art, architecture, or design you gravitate toward.

15. Reflect upon an extreme success or failure you experienced.

16. Contemplate any messages you internalize about yourself.

17. Evaluate your interactions with animals, both wild and domestic.

18. Review the authority figures from your past and the current hierarchical frameworks that are impacting you.

19. Reflect upon what you shy away or disengage from.

20. Describe what you value.

This list isn't intended to be exhaustive, nor is it intended to pinpoint specific periods of time in your life. You may find something historically relevant to you, or it might be from this present moment. Note also that the list was created to be as open as possible without labeling the influencing factors as good or bad. Doing so allows a broader stream of consciousness by which to determine your attitudes regarding conflict. Remember that our internal state is what guides our external manifestations, as is the case with many medical conditions. Recently someone shared that one of their three children was diagnosed with Type 1 diabetes, a serious condition that affected the way their daughter was raised. Her diabetes eventually bled into other areas of the child's upbringing. In time the siblings grew resentful because of the perceived inequity in the way they were raised. As young adults, this is now a source of underlying conflict. What started as a relatively common medical diagnosis became a present-day conflict script. At face value, the medical condition wasn't the source of the conflict. Rather, it was how the diagnosis shaped the family environment, parenting styles, and lived experiences for all of the children. Furthermore, to state that the diabetes only impacted the one child would be short-sighted. The diagnosis became a lived experience for everyone within the household, and the theme of "equity versus equality" became the crux of family conflict.

"Equity versus equality" isn't my tipping point. For me, advocacy for those who need to be heard is a strong trigger. Ensuring that people are heard is part of my emotional DNA; it's almost impossible to remove this from my identity. Initially, I thought this was because of my lifelong battle with significant auditory issues. This is an easy conclusion to draw given the number of ear surgeries I had in the past and the continual hearing loss I still endure. However, it was a recent revelation that created more understanding of this theme. Growing up, my family discussed how "Little Kiley" would have temper tantrums so severe I would be placed on the curb outside my home. Eventually I would simmer down and be brought back inside. The present-day joking focuses on my intense tantrums, but there isn't much conversation about how things might have been different if my family had been more aware that my ongoing frustration stemmed from not being able to physically hear well. Because they weren't cognizant of these hearing issues, the message I internalized was a requirement to give them a hall-pass for schlepping me outside during a childhood outburst. Even into adulthood, I didn't think I had permission to feel badly about the way my family shared these experiences with others. Because it was conveyed that everyone involved was doing their best in those circumstances, it seemed unfair for me to be critical of anyone. Now I understand that my grief and heartache is for the little girl who was hurting and alone on the curb. Regardless of my family's intentions, the impact was my shame and embarrassment for something outside of my control. No wonder advocacy for the unheard is so prevalent in my conflict script. Because time and maturity are now on my side, I am aware that I can feel personally sad about something without vilifying others who had no ill intentions.

Starting with a wide, exploratory lens helps create the broadest level of understanding about that which may be impacting the conflict script. Subtexts can be unveiled when the largest platforms are deliberately assessed. The medical crises of childhood diabetes and ruptured ear drums were the catalyst for shaping the conflict script. This is why it's so important to be expansive when evaluating the experiences that potentially shape your conflict script, and just because something is impactful for one person doesn't guarantee it will be for another. Even a simple hobby, activity, or interest can have a huge bearing on a person's conflict script if it has been strongly incorporated into their worldview.

Consider the example of the mediator who spoke in-depth about hockey and Wayne Gretzky. It doesn't have to be my perspective for it to have weight and meaning. Therefore, it's important not to discount areas that might seem superficial at first glance. Just because a person hasn't weathered a catastrophic business dispute, major medical condition, or a security issue like poverty or abuse doesn't mean they don't have a deep perspective on conflict. In fact, some people with more harmonious backgrounds have profound conflict scripts because of what has filtered into them. If you struggle to identify your conflict scripts, it's often beneficial to mentally exaggerate past experiences to help remember details and create understanding. The practice of intentional exaggeration can bring aspects to light that help inform what is impactful.

A handful of people can be asked to photograph the same subject, and the picture captured will be different for each one. Each photographer will decide what to focus on, what to put in the background, the lighting used, the clarity desired, and the preferred snapshot size. In this analogy, the printed photograph represents the imagery tied to the conflict script, the photographed subject matter represents conflict, and the camera represents the Conflict Imagery Charting Model.

The camera and photography process represent going through the
Conflict Imagery Charting Model.

A flag represents the chosen mental subject of conflict the
photographer wishes to capture for the viewer to see in a photograph.

The finalized and printed photograph of flags represents the unique
conflict imagery projected to the world by the photographer.

The camera is only useful if it's put to use, so the process of picking up the device and deciding to take a picture and finally developing it into a tangible print represents how our unique, internalized conflict script is manifested into an external image that can be shared. In this example, the flags are photographed blowing in the wind. This is my stepdad's photograph, and his creative eye shares his experience and feelings about living in Senegal, Africa. Someone else, however, might have decided to photograph the flags during a storm, at night, or when the winds were still. The subject matter alone, in this case a flag, isn't enough to tell the whole story. It comes to life when it's captured in the way the photographer intends. The photograph then becomes a vessel enabling the viewer to understand and embrace the lived experiences, feelings, and beliefs of the photographer. This is why two different photographers will never produce the exact same photograph, even if the intended subject matter is the same.

Imagery serves as a channel to create understanding, awareness, and dialogue about viewpoints on conflict scripts and helps normalize conversations about conflict. In turn, empathy, compassion, and identification is cultivated among opposing parties. The process of identifying and naming something has the power to deal with and influence associated fears, misunderstandings, confusion, and distress. Allowing ourselves to become authoritative puzzle-makers and picture-takers of conflict through the discovery and identification of our unique conflict scripts results in valuable imagery that I hope can help improve the world.

Imagery Touchpoints:

1. Complete the Biographical Conflict Information Identification exercise. What material or insights stand out to you that help reveal evidence about your conflict script and how and why it may have formed the way it did?

2. Think about a time when you assembled a puzzle or took a meaningful photograph. What went into that process? How did you begin? How could you apply the same approach to identifying your conflict script?

3. Open up your cell phone and choose a picture that tells a story. What story does it tell, and how did you go about capturing that story? What did you decide to focus on, and what did you edit out of the final photo?

Imagery Snapshot: *Building an awareness of the experiences that influence your conflict script will allow you to identify the best imagery through which to share those experiences with the world. Identifying the components that influence your conflict script helps create awareness that will allow you to determine the external manifestations of the imagery constructs and depictions of them you wish to share with the world.*

What Does a Musk Ox
Have to do With Anything?

Once conflict scripts and subtexts have been named and personalized, they can serve as a tool for creating tangible, outward manifestations of these internal constructs through the use of imagery and imagination. In other words, your imagery and imagination about conflict now has purpose and direction that can thereby create understanding. This understanding is two-fold and will be evident through your growing self-compassion and self-empathy, while others will gain insights on your perspective of conflict. How, then, should this imagery be externalized? Many people get stuck at this point in the process because they assume there is a right and wrong way of projecting an image or association regarding conflict. Approaching conflict with a more neutral mindset and considering it as just one facet of our existence gives us permission to see many options. As I've demonstrated through these many personality exercises, imagery, too, can be projected in a variety of ways.

Imagery and imagination are essentially the way we objectively externalize the subjective or internal. For some, this imagery might be a picture or symbol. For others, it could be an analogy or statement. I mentioned earlier that one of my life themes is advocacy for those I feel should be heard. The external symbol of hearing is a representation of my internal desire to ensure people have a voice. This belief strongly impacts my conflict scripts, which is why it's so important that the imagery I use conveys this. Few who know me would be surprised to learn that I identify with the lioness. In fact, my younger brother has a tattoo of a lion to symbolize me. If you find yourself connecting with a particular phrase, color, event, symbol, song, or picture, think about why it holds meaning for you. It's likely a key to how you might view the management of conflict. Study your lifestyle: the car you drive, the house you live in, the clothes you wear, the way you spend your free time. These are big indicators of personal values, and these tenets contribute to the way we interact with others. These interactions serve as guideposts to our conflict management philosophies. Once we understand these internal pillars, we then can name them in a way that allows others to better understand our perspective.

Give yourself permission to take time and care to navigate the imagery naming process because it can be difficult to articulate the nebulous. With our chosen imagery platform, we have a basis for future understanding and dialogue. I may not be able to find all the words to fully articulate why advocacy for the unheard is important to me and that it plays a large role in how I deal with conflict, but when I simply state that one of my conflict imageries is a lioness, it instantly conveys something to others that they can understand. For the mediators who participated in my dissertation study, the use of analogies helped articulate their conflict management philosophies. Furthermore, the more common a lived experience is, the more likely it will connect with a broad audience. For example, it's no stretch to say that most everyone knows what a lioness is. It's such a common fixture in art, religion, culture, zoos, and books, that almost everyone would know what I'm saying when I indicate that my conflict management style has components of a lioness tied to it. If an uncommon animal was used to create my conflict imagery, however, the image might be less successful. For instance, a musk ox is also a strong and protective mammal. In fact, it is considered by many to be one of the top fifteen most protective animals on the planet.[33] As a symbol for protectiveness, however, it's used far less widely. While I could still choose to use the musk ox instead of a lioness to portray my protective personality trait, the imagery connection is much stronger with the lioness.

This is not to dissuade the use of less-common images if there is a strong personal association to them, but it's also important to consider whether the image will resonate with the intended audience. After all, the goal is to help create external symbols for internal states of being. If the imagery doesn't connect with others, it fails to achieve the intended goal—better understanding among people about internal conflict scripts and subtexts. This is why scenes from famous movies, lines from popular poetry, lyrics from celebrated songs, and references to prominent artwork are continually used to relay messages to others. Assigning the same thought process to conflict scripts helps address the fear, stigma, and angst that is often tied to conversations about conflict. Imagery informed by conflict scripts and subtexts helps normalize the dialogue. When something is normalized, it's more recognized and embraced in mainstream interactions.

Look at past taboos that have become common cultural placeholders in modern society—the topic of sex and sexuality, for instance. There was a period of time when conversations about sex were prohibited or frowned upon. Now, sex is a topic found in many newspaper articles, movies, and song lyrics. When something is routinely addressed, it gets staying power. Imagery is a method for transporting people between external awareness and an internal state. The intended outcome is the reduction of complexity in conveying internal states. The practice of articulating imagery is like watching for the tip of an iceberg to reveal what lies beneath the ocean's surface. The tip of the iceberg isn't powerful, but it is an extremely important marker, tool, and reference point. Also, the tip of the iceberg isn't the only means of locating what exists below the surface of the ocean. Similarly, the imagery tool you decide to use to convey your conflict script isn't the only tool you can use in your conflict management approach, but it can be a highly powerful and effective resource.

Furthermore, the image you choose doesn't have to be heavy or philosophical to effectively illustrate your conflict script. In fact, many people have less-complicated views on conflict than I. If the world was full of musk oxen and lionesses, the survival of the planet would be in jeopardy because the population would fail to grow. Recently, I learned through a conversation with my mom that someone had described her as the "eye of the storm." While the reference is to hurricanes, it instantly created meaning for me because tornadoes and extreme weather are a reality for Midwesterners. During a hurricane, the winds spin violently, but the eye, or center, of the storm remains still and calm. A better description might not exist to describe my mom. She has a remarkable ability to ground herself even when tumult and chaos ensues. The "eye of the storm" image is a fabulous way to externally express this. You don't have to meet my mom to have a better understanding of her personality.

Upon discovering that my mom had been described this way, it seemed worthwhile to learn whether other people had similar experiences naming something tied to their expressions during conflict. The mediators I interviewed hadn't been explicitly asked to identify their conflict scripts or imageries, but they had naturally done so of their own accord. So for this informal assessment, I asked a handful of family and friends to answer the following question: "If you had to describe your approach to conflict using a symbol, color, image, quote, lyric, sport, artwork, etc., what would it be?" My intention was to present a question in a conversational way to determine whether normalizing conversation surrounding conflict elicited any specific feedback. Here's what I found:

- During conflict, I fit puzzle pieces together.

- I am the color red during conflict.

- During conflict, I am a flat body of water—calm.

- I associate conflict with fireworks. Fireworks can be scary, must be handled carefully, each viewer has different "favorites," and beauty can result from all the noise and chaos.

- Conflict is like walking on a tightrope from one point to another. It's also like volleyball, where there is a great deal of back and forth.

- The image of a bridge comes to mind when thinking about conflict.

- My approach to conflict is like owning a Swiss Army Knife. You never know which tool you might need because every situation is different.

- Diamonds are what come to mind because conflict feels like a lot of pressure.

It's interesting that expressions like fireworks, water, volleyball, multi-tooled knives, diamonds, tightropes, and puzzles were used by people as their conflict imageries. No two people provided the same example, and not one person used the lioness as an image. This demonstrates the importance of recognizing that imagery is unique to each individual. I may be the lioness, but it certainly doesn't mean that anyone else needs to be. Because I know each of these people closely, it was fascinating to discover their self-identifying images. The person who described themselves as calm, flat water provided one of the most accurate and insightful portrayals of their conflict interactions. This man is the most grounded and unflappable person I know. Yet, I wouldn't have thought of the calm, flat water image if I was asked to identify his conflict management approach. It was perfect. Allowing him to self-identify provided far more vision than I could have ever delivered. It was spot on. He also happens to be a man who enjoys fishing as a hobby, so it's logical that his conflict script and imagery is tied to his lived experience with water. Most of us can imagine standing by a perfectly still lake. Close your eyes and picture it. Now you have a better idea of how he approaches conflict. He is the embodiment of stability. Stillness. Calm. He also happens to be my remarkable older brother.

On the other hand, I was initially very surprised when I learned that one individual connected with the imagery of fireworks because that isn't the first association I make when I think about her approach to conflict. The explanation she provided, however, made it crystal clear to me. When I think about fireworks, the explosive and loud nature is what comes to mind. This isn't how I would describe this person. Instead, I would call her a blend of whimsy and wisdom. When she later stated that she believed "fireworks can be scary, must be handled carefully, each viewer has different 'favorites,' and beauty can result from all the noise and chaos," I quickly understood her perspective. Isn't her expression both whimsical and wise? She didn't say she was noisy or chaotic. Instead, she described the creative outcomes that can result from the noise and chaos of fireworks. Knowing her personal background, it's such a fitting picture for how she has dealt with the immense adversity she has faced. Now I understand the whimsy and wisdom of her fireworks. They aren't supposed to be my fireworks; they are hers.

Another example that was initially surprising to me was the reference to a diamond. The person who offered this depiction could be described as logical, linear, and concrete in his communication style. The symbol of the diamond struck me as rather curious because I associate opulence with diamonds. When I probed him about the diamond imagery, he said he feels conflict can be high pressure, and he knows that diamonds are produced through the process of intense heat and force. He indicated that other high-pressure images came to his mind when he thought about conflict, but it was the diamond that spoke to him. He didn't share with me that diamonds are expensive or sparkly. Those were my associations with diamonds. Rather, he associated with the way in which diamonds are created. Upon hearing his perspective, I understood why it carried meaning for him. The logical and methodical aspects of his personality were unveiled when he was allowed to share why he'd selected the diamond imagery. When people are allowed to self-identify and self-define, a clearer picture appears. It's important to get out of the way and let people do more of the exploring, talking, and revealing. It can be easy to fall for the trap of filling in the blanks for others, which then become our narratives, and we need the narrative to be theirs. These insights belong to my talented younger brother, and he is certainly capable of voicing his story without the help of his older sister.

If we are unclear about someone's self-identified imagery, we can ask them to define it. For example, maybe I eventually decide that the musk ox is better than a lioness to describe my conflict imagery. To fully appreciate the imagery, however, might require someone to gain a fuller understanding of the musk ox. The example of the fireworks required more information on the symbol they provided. Once

I understood their perspective, it gave me greater insights into the way they saw themselves. In the case of the Swiss Army Knife, I appreciated the description of a knife as a multi-faceted tool rather than a weapon. This individual also sent me a picture of the knife they had visualized, and so did the person who invoked tight-rope walking for their conflict imagery. As a visual learner, this was a great way for me to better understand their symbolism. I hadn't asked for pictures, but they went a long way for me gaining insights into their thoughts. See below:

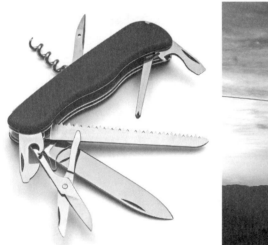 

Having known the person who used the volleyball image for almost twenty years, it was a fitting symbol she provided. She frequently uses the phrase "playing devil's advocate" when encouraging people to see another viewpoint. It's her technique for priming the listener to prepare to learn about the other side of the discussion. She will then proceed to consider the flip side to the issue at hand, but it's never done in a combative way. Rather, she uses the discourse as an opportunity to add another perspective on the issue, a habit that aligns well with her volleyball analogy—her nature is to volley a topic back and forth while it's under consideration. I almost chuckle now when I hear anyone use the phrase because I so strongly associate my dear friend with this expression.

The man who used the color red to describe his conflict management style was also highly accurate. Ironically, an employee of his once told me that his staff would text the words "code red" to each other if they knew he was in a particular mindset that might make a conflict more challenging. "Code red" signals the potential for imminent tumult and to therefore stay on high alert. Red is also a universal color for heat, which certainly keeps with the way he tends to deal with conflict. He comes in hot and often burns things down along the way, which stands in stark contrast to the calm body of water analogy previously discussed. Both are accurate, and there's no judgement from me about the effectiveness of either style or approach. Both heat and calm are needed in this world. My goal is to identify, label, and normalize communication about conflict scripts and imagery. Once this is done, people can determine their own level of comfort with their self-identified imagery. A musk ox or a lioness might represent my approach to conflict management, and only I can decide how to be the zookeeper of these fiercely protective wildlife.

Imagery Touchpoints:

1. Ask yourself, "If I had to describe my approach to conflict using a symbol, color, image, quote, lyric, sport, work of art, etc., what would it be?" Consider doing an internet search for the word or phrase you identified to solidify that image in your mind.

2. Think about a time you were looking at a menu and didn't know what an option was by the title alone. How did you learn the ingredients? Was there a picture of the dish or a brief description provided? Did you ask your server for details? Similarly, consider how the use of conflict imagery on its own can be problematic if context isn't provided along with it.

3. How have your thoughts about your conflict imagery changed or remained the same in light of the examples provided by those around you or those offered in this book? Survey a few people in your life to see how they answer question #1 above. Ask people to elaborate on their responses if any of their imagery surprises you given what you know about them. Seek to truly understand how they reached their chosen imagery.

Imagery Snapshot: *The self-identification and definition of the conflict imagery a person selects is important. Allow exploration and communication about the process of embracing conflict imagery to enrich context and meaning.*

Square Peg in a Round Hole

If a phrase has been in continual use since the 1800s, it's clearly literary gold. When Sydney Smith gave a series of speeches at the Royal Institution, he used imagery to help the audience better understand moral philosophy:

> *If you choose to represent the various parts in life by holes upon a table of different shapes—some circular, some triangular, some square, some oblong—and the person acting these parts by bits of wood of similar shapes, we shall generally find that the triangular person has got into the square hole, the oblong into the triangular, and a square person has squeezed himself into the round hole. The officer and the office, the doer and the thing done, seldom fit so exactly, that we can say they were almost made for each other.*[34]

A square peg in a round hole. Sydney Smith was wise enough to use metaphors to help delineate and simplify the concept of what happens when disparate facets of life are forced together. We frequently use the expression "a square peg in a round hole" to help people visualize when two things cannot be perfectly resolved. Most people visualize that a square peg cannot fit at all into a round hole much in the same way that oil and water never fully emulsify. However, if you read the full paragraph, this isn't exactly what Smith was stating. Let's unpack the para-  graph. The various shapes do manage to fit into different shaped holes, but typically it is an irregular alignment because the positioning of one shape doesn't fully fill the space of a different shape. Hence, the phrase "square peg in a round hole" has evolved to signify a faulty design, and today the expression is used in many training environments. Much of the human resources or business advice about personality types states that people, especially leaders, shouldn't attempt to place a square peg into a round hole. We assume the two are incompatible and that the square peg is too big to fit. Take a moment and conduct a quick internet search for the idiom, and you'll find many representations of this paradigm—the peg and the hole remain apart from each other, not conjoined in any fashion. However, sometimes life is more complicated than this, and fitting squares into circles is the only available option, so can this peg-and-hole scheme actually work?

Maybe we need to stop visualizing the children's toy where the goal is to use the wooden mallet to whack various shapes through the matching holes. It creates the false illusion that life is about a one-to-one, perfectly aligned fit. If you've lived longer than a nanosecond, however, you know this isn't always realistic or feasible. Furthermore, it wouldn't even be productive to live in a world where pieces sail through openings with no friction. The visualization of the square peg in a round hole trips people up because we assume the square peg is always larger than the

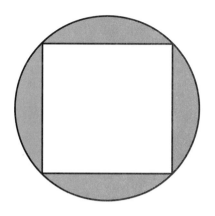

round hole so it has to be jammed through or the edges of the round peg have to be chiseled or sanded away. It's hard to remember that if you were to slip a square peg into a round hole it could fit into, about 65 percent of the space would be filled.[35] Not a perfect fit by any measure, but what if the remaining 35 percent of open space, of inexactitude, was acceptable?

What about a round peg in a square hole, another attempt at uniting two incompatibles? This question can best be answered using Pythagoras' Theorem to evaluate the ratios involved. In this case, about 22 percent of the space is open between the peg and hole. While this model reduces the amount of open

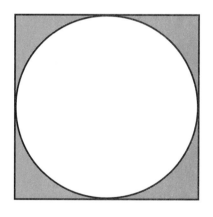

space, the peg still isn't a perfect fit. It's considered an absolute mismatch by many accounts.

What if a little space, a little wiggle room between ill-fitting shapes, wasn't a mistake? What if shapes don't have to be a perfect match to co-exist? Case in point, in the 1800s, Dutch settlers built

barns using squared pegs pre-
cisely inserted into round
holes. It was an extremely
laborious process where the
squared, octagonal treenails
were hand-carved to fit inside
round holes. The pegs were
squared due to the shape of
the drawknife, the tool used
to create them. Architect and

New World Dutch barn expert John Fitchen observed and docu-
mented the strength of this architecture during an attempt to demolish
one of these Dutch barns.[36] The farmer who was going to remove the
barn thought it would be a standard demolition project, but when it
came time to bring it down, the structure wouldn't dislodge. On
further inspection, they discovered that this seemingly mis-matched
peg-in-hole method had created a permanent structure; the squared
pegs acted as gripping teeth inside the round opening. Were they the
same shape, the pegs could wriggle free of the holes, weakening the
structure over time. Look at how modern drywall nails shimmy out
after many years. This isn't the case with New World Dutch barns.
In fact, after discovering how the barn was held together, the demolition team had to painstakingly remove every joint by manually
sawing them apart one at a time. It was a long and arduous process
and certainly a lesson in the effectiveness of a non-traditional building method. Although the time and cost efficiency of steel eventually
replaced the wooden treenail design, the fact that these antique barns
still stand is testament to the ingenuity of unconventional thinking.

While the goal of this design was to create a permanent bond
between the peg and hole, the partnership this imagery demonstrates
also makes sense in other situations. We may think that 22 to 35

percent of open space is a failed design because we want 100 percent of the peg and hole to fit together. However, we might want air or water to pass through or light to shine in. Fully plugging a hole shouldn't always be the goal, and this unconventional structure can be beneficial in many other circumstances. The fruit and vegetable crisper drawers in the refrigerator are a great example. Produce is kept fresh longer with an airflow that maintains the right level of humidity. An airtight seal isn't ideal for the longevity of produce.

Attics are another example. Trapped moisture is the arch-nemesis of ceilings, so allowing moisture to escape prevents damaging condensation. This is why homes are designed with vents located in strategic places throughout the house. The same logic holds true for sunglasses. The goal isn't to remove 100 percent of the sun's rays or to cancel the entry of all light. Instead, sunglasses are designed to reduce harmful UV rays and brightness that makes it difficult to see clearly. In each of these situations, removing every bit of air, water, or light isn't the intention; it's finding a balance. The Dutch were aiming for a harmonious balance between structural integrity and space between treenail and hole. The design built strong, enduring structures that proved to be nearly indestructible.

These imagery examples teach the importance of schemes that strike a harmony between disparate shapes (or in our case, personalities) to create definitive and effective results. These designs aren't exclusionary or punitive; they're simply pieces of engineering that serve the greater good. Someone could look at the Dutch barn structures and believe the pegs were placed in error because gaps exist in the peg-hole design. If we do the same with our personal lives and believe there needs to be a perfect fit to handle conflict effectively, we will inevitably reduce our openness to ideas that don't appear to fit the norm. And we might miss some of the added benefits resulting from atypical approaches. Once you've deeply and sincerely explored your background, philosophy, and approach to conflict, embrace a similar attitude to the Dutch barn builders. Use this information to determine the internalized conflict scripts you wish to manifest externally in the imagery you express to others. The goal is to authentically design your imagery of conflict management and not get weighed down by pressure to conform. This can be for anyone with whom you might benefit from finding balance and harmony— family, colleagues, friends, bosses, or organizational members. After all, these relationships are where the "square peg in a round hole" most likely exist. Just like the Dutch barn, a solid structure can be built without any one part having to entirely give way to another.

The Dutch treenail, crisper drawer, house vent, and sunglasses all represent how an adaptable design can achieve ideal outcomes. Our goal isn't to fight against external factors but to create internal structures that produce the gripping, ventilating, and filtering power for success. The barn, refrigerator, house, and sun aren't being asked to change what they are. Instead, the treenail, crisper, vent, and glasses are all adaptive tools that create greater harmony that fosters productivity, efficiency, and competency. They are part of a greater whole. Your relationships pertaining to conflict management will reap the benefits of framing the larger picture. Remind yourself that your imagery expression is intended to unveil an effective tool for you to use when faced with external factors. It is both adaptable and authentic.

Your imagery is not an attempt to change others around you. It is a tool to help yourself and others remember that the square peg and round hole are not incompatible, and one does not need to out-muscle the other. The goal is to convey a message about your conflict management approach. This allows others to better understand your nature, and it provides a method for you to better understand yourself. You can then use this reciprocal and iterative process as a catalyst for deeper conversations with people through the process of acceptance. When we start giving permission for people to be square pegs and round holes, we spend less time trying to aggressively chisel away at ourselves and others. We become more mindful and affirming of natural states of being. The result is the refinement of our personality.

This honing begins with you. Once you have determined your conflict imagery expression, be prepared for not everyone to understand or embrace it. It isn't their expression to own any more than their expression is yours to own. The square peg, round hole analogy should create a mindset of comfort with our individual conflict management style. Imagery expression is simply an external manifestation of our internal state, and none of us can take ownership or responsibility for someone else's internal welfare. Conversely, other people aren't accountable for our internal health. However, imagery expression can serve as an effective therapeutic tool because as we express and project our internal state in an honest way, we gain more understanding of ourselves and master the way we respond to stimuli. Through the process of identifying our conflict imagery expression and learning about those others wish to share, we glean insights about how to refine ourselves in ways that feel authentic. Additionally, we can gather information about others that allows us to become more malleable in our interactions with them. The square pegs and round holes don't need to break. Instead, they can bend.

Imagery Touchpoints:

1. What initially comes to mind when you think of the saying, "Trying to fit a square peg in a round hole?" How has this chapter altered your perspective?

2. Give other examples of objects intended to allow some degree of air, light, or water to pass through. The Dutch treenail, refrigerator crisper, house vents, and sunglasses were already offered as illustrations, so consider others.

3. Role-play how you might respond once you share your conflict imagery expression with others. What will you do in instances where your expression doesn't seem to align with that of others?

Imagery Snapshot: *Conflict imagery expression is a tool to create more collaborative understanding through which we can refine ourselves without needing to become defensive. It simply becomes an avenue for self-discovery and communication for future malleability and contemplation.*

Diamonds Are a Girl's Best Friend

Diamonds are remarkable because they have such humble beginnings. As we examined earlier in the book, someone I surveyed associated conflict management with diamonds because of the process by which they are created—through heat and pressure—but maybe a lesser-known fact is that diamonds can now be produced in labs. These manufactured diamonds, however, do not have the same raw characteristics that occur through the natural process. Natural diamonds are created hundreds of feet underground in specific parts of the world over the course of thousands of years through the pressurization of natural carbon. The result is a brilliant stone.

One of the most valuable diamond mines in the world, Jwaneng of Botswana, is more than 2,000 feet below ground and touches 15 million diamond carats each year.[37] Incredible resources are poured into these dangerous mines because they unearth these rare gemstones. Natural diamonds are a finite resource with unique characteristics where no two natural diamonds look the same. Someone could buy a lab-created diamond and get a shimmery stone, but it would lack the irregularities formed only by the hands of nature. If you are holding a natural diamond, you are holding some of the oldest and strongest naturally occurring minerals on the planet. Tough, beautiful, long-lasting, and useful. Who wouldn't want to be described this way?

When Marilyn Monroe sang that "diamonds are a girl's best friend," the focus was on the titillating aspects of her performance. However, many of the other lyrics have great life lessons, as in "time rolls on" and "these rocks don't lose their shape." In other words, despite what changes in the world, the diamond is unwavering. No wonder diamonds are used both in engagement ring settings and in industry for polishing, drilling, and cutting—form and function coming together in an idyllic fashion. After a bit of research, it now makes sense to me why that surveyed individual decided the diamond was a good representation of their conflict management philosophy: pressure often results in strong outcomes.

One of the aspects that makes a diamond special is that no two naturally occurring diamonds are the same, because the inclusions found within the diamond are what make it unique. Some jewelers maintain that the characteristics of a diamond are basically the internal birthmarks of the stone. What is found within the diamond is what impacts how the diamond will externally shine. This is a great metaphor for the human condition. Inclusions in and of themselves are not problematic to the diamond, but the type and size can affect its brilliance. The cut and polish can yield the best results given the type of inclusions found within the gem. Our personalities are very similar. Sometimes the right type of polishing and honing will elicit the best from us.

Recently, I was asked to update a training curriculum that would be used during a succession planning workshop. What kept stumping me was that the audience knew their direction (succession planning), but their momentum slowed once the process began, and few fully completed the planning. Every business operator knows that succession planning is useful and necessary, so the lack of follow-through was baffling even to them. Upon reflection, though, I realized that this succession planning dilemma isn't unusual. In many facets of life, we know the best intention and direction we seek, but we fail to see it through to fruition. For example, most people would say that nutrition, sleep, and exercise are good behaviors. Most people would say that smoking, stressful living, and excessive screen time are markers of an unhealthy lifestyle. So if we know what's good for us, why do we resist? This was the crux of the curriculum revision problem.

Consider your own life and the disconnections between what you would like to happen and what you actually do. One area I wrestle with is establishing healthy sleep patterns. I know it's better for me, but I allow other aspects of life to trump slumber. By looking at our own thoughts and behaviors, we are better equipped to help others address their goals compassionately and creatively.

It struck me that this was an ideal opportunity to use imagery as an avenue to help participants move beyond the impasse they were facing. Similar to having issues with conflict, many people get stuck when they deal with challenging situations. Most people don't relish living in a continual state of conflict, but many don't know how to move forward in a constructive manner. In both succession planning and conflict management, the parties know their desired direction. This isn't the issue. The issue is charting a path that creates momentum to achieve results. Through revamping this aspect of the succession planning curriculum, I created the Direction Imaging Diagram with the Direction Diamond as a supplemental visual aid. In essence, it's a flow chart that helps provide clarity on the issues that need to be addressed. These concepts aren't new, but what was helpful to the participants were the visual cues that keep them focused and intentional with their efforts. Additionally, these models helped create a framework for the practitioners facilitating the conversations. Creating language for the process helps keep behaviors active, which often resolves the impasse.

The training resources are presented below, so take a moment to review them. It's no coincidence that the materials use words starting with the letter D throughout the handout, or that the descriptors of these words all rhyme (e.g. evaluate; contemplate; communicate; activate). Mental maps are most successful when they're easy to remember, when the association is strong, and when the information is meaningful. The last thing we want an eager audience to experience is the weight of a laborious process. If anything, the process should elevate them to a place where they feel empowered, informed, and confident in their abilities. We want people to leave our presence with a heightened ability to function on their own. Life is full of opportunities to process difficult circumstances, so it's best if we can impart usable and transferable skill sets for ongoing practice. It's not overly helpful to support individuals during a conflict situation without guidance on how to transfer the lessons to other facets of their lives. Hence, the Direction Imaging Diagram and Direction Diamond were born. Study the concepts to determine the various ways the materials could be utilized in the real world. The potential is endless as there are always mountains to climb that require our ability to follow through.

DIRECTION IMAGING

Guided imagery facilitates exploration of holistic options.

DESIGNING THE DIRECTION DIAMOND

The Direction Diamond is a helpful visual for charting how to create the momentum and energy for attaining a desired result.

Following the imagery of the diamond allows participants to pause, assess, and regroup both individually and collectively so that this iterative process is thoughtful, practical, and collaborative. In doing so, the "direction path" is designed and acted upon to achieve organized, measurable, and sustainable results.

THE **FOUR D'S** OF THE DIRECTION DIAMOND

DETERMINE
evaluate

- Neutrally assess the given dynamics.
- Explore and anticipate all possible options.
- Play scenarios out to the end.
- Consider who and what should be involved.
- Think through what can or cannot be controlled.
- Reality-test choices and consequences.

DECIDE
contemplate

- Chart the required trajectory.
- Ponder the intent and impact of choices.
- Weigh if selections are realistic and measurable.
- Guage what should remain or be removed for continued consideration.
- Strategize the accountability variables.
- Define the commitment to inclusion and exclusion of decisions.

DECLARE
communicate

- Articulate the desired intent, impact, and outcomes.
- Strive for shared understanding among parties.
- Clarify, reframe, and mirror when it is appropriate.
- Create sustainable accountability plans.
- Memorialize in writing when it is feasible.
- Use open, affirming, and authentic dialogue.

DELIVER
activate

- Give and receive according to parameters.
- Engage and act upon commitments.
- Manifest internal and external boundaries.
- Operate with specificity and purpose.
- Exercise the conditions and steps of the plan.
- Fulfill and complete goals and outcomes.

All of the "D's" are critical for creating direction. However, the time, energy, and resources spent at each point in the cycle might vary depending on the specifics of the situation and parties involved. While this is a structured guide, a degree of organic flexibility and intuition should be utilized to foster authentic empowerment.

Upon assessing the materials from a variety of perspectives with several real-life experiences you have encountered, consider questions to develop your reflection skills. Questions could be along the lines of:

1. Which of the four "D's" do you find yourself naturally inclined to process? Why do you think that might be?

2. Are there certain "D's" you seem to avoid? What sense do you have about why this is?

3. How will you deal with the areas where processing and moving forward might be difficult? How will you assess progress? How will you reward accomplishments?

4. What type of schedule will you create to ensure regular check-ins and maintenance?

After studying this diagram, you may decide to create your own model that aligns with your conflict management paradigm and philosophy. That's great! The most efficient way to become an effective practitioner is to utilize a platform that feels innate. It's just important to incorporate an element of imagery into your resources so you can demonstrate the very components you're trying to instill in those navigating conflict. So far, you have been provided examples such as the home renovation toolbox, the Diamond Diagram, Seatbelt Kiley, and the lionness vs. musk ox to describe the elements of conflict management that resonate with me. These became part of my practice through intentional self-reflection, feedback from trusted individuals in my life, and studying the wisdom of experts. I would encourage you to do the same. You will likely find that the language and concepts regarding your conflict management approach will come to light during your exploration. Once this happens, you'll be in a stronger place to help others with their own conflict management journey. You will become like the diamond with its own unique birthmark inclusions with enough strength to build the world around it. Just like a brilliant diamond, when shaped properly you will shine brightly.

Imagery Touchpoints:

1. Study the Direction Imaging Diagram and Direction Diamond to see how the materials fit into your conflict management style. How could you integrate this into your practice?

2. What are some of the personal barriers you have experienced when attempting to navigate something challenging? How might these experiences translate into information you could use to help others experiencing the obstacles involved in conflict management?

3. What types of visual aids have you found most useful when moving through a situation where you know your intended direction? How might you create your own materials that incorporate an element of imagery to use when helping others navigate conflict?

Imagery Snapshot: *Useful tools stem from a level of comfort and familiarity with the content and materials. Self-reflection, input from personal relationships, and wisdom from experts can help create and shape the mechanics selected during conflict management. The Direction Imaging Diagram and Direction Diamond are examples of the resulting manifestations from the practice of creating a meaningful platform.*

The Devil's in the Details

Determining an imagery model requires a bit of detective work, investigating both the self and the observations of others. We have already established that an effective image must resonate both with the individual and the audience. It requires a delicate balance for the process and outcomes to be authentic and enduring. Like any detective work, we must assess this information through clues and cues. In the 1800s, German-born architect Ludwig Mies van der Rohe coined the phrase "God is in the details" (which eventually led to the modern "the devil's in the details") to shed light on the importance of paying attention to our surroundings and to teach people about the quest for truth. He believed that truth was often found through the observation and analysis of minute attributes.[38] Nothing should be left to chance if the goal was creating a foundation of truth.

The search for your conflict management imagery is a quest for your own personal truth. Eliciting it in others is part of the responsibility of a conflict manager, whether in a professional capacity or as a layman seeking best practices for working through the variables of daily conflict. Helping people find their own conflict management imagery is the pinnacle of success for anyone striving to make conflict management a meaningful and insightful voyage. People will provide external clues about their internal make-up. It just takes detective skills to analyze what they provide. It isn't often delivered overtly, as the information people provide about themselves tends to be more nuanced.

When studying people, consider the subtleties of their language:

1. What expressions do they use?

   "When I was a child…"

   "I'm going to play devil's advocate here…"

2. What analogies do they provide?

   "It's a burr in my saddle when…"

   "It fills my bucket when…"

3. How do they use body language?

   They cross their arms when a new topic is presented.

   They bite their nails when they're nervous.

4. What interests do they mention?

   "I enjoy woodworking in my garage…"

   "I like taking yoga classes…"

5. How do they spend their free time?

   She goes to her lake home every weekend.

   He tinkers on his vintage motorcycle.

6. What hobbies do they engage in?

   He takes photography classes at the community college.

   She is part of a book club.

7. What career paths have they taken?

    She has been a banker, homemaker, executive administrator...

    He has been a teacher, coach, store manager...

8. What activities do they enjoy?

    He likes to hike outdoors.

    She likes to cross-stitch.

9. How do they interact with friends?

    Their home is always open to guests.

    He is part of a Bible study.

10. What life experiences have they undertaken?

    She has lived in thirteen different states as a military child.

    He ruined his knees in a skiing accident.

11. How do they engage with family?

    She only attends the obligatory family events.

    He reads to his children every night.

12. What disconnections do you observe between their words and actions?

    He says he wants to lose weight and then eats fast food almost daily.

    She says she wants to save money and shops at the mall every weekend.

13. What are the sources of information they use?

    She watches Fox News regularly.

    He reads the local newspaper for political insights.

14. How do they behave in professional settings?

> She pauses before providing any feedback to her boss.
>
> He is defensive when coworkers question the data he reports.

15. What successes have you observed in their lives?

> He played basketball in college.
>
> She plays the violin with a local band.

16. What messages do they repeat?

> "My father never…"
>
> "I know I've said this before, but…"

17. What types of interactions do they avoid?

> She seems to avoid conversations with authority figures.
>
> He appears to withdraw when he's asked about complex emotions.

18. How do they deal with challenges?

> He tends to retreat quietly when there are obstacles.
>
> She demonstrates a lot of grit and tenacity during difficult times.

19. What belief systems do they espouse?

> "If it ain't broke, don't fix it."
>
> "At all costs, you should always follow through on a commitment."

20. What goals have they articulated?

> "I want to retire in Florida by the water."
>
> "I want to be entirely debt-free to help my kids with college expenses."

21. What failures have you witnessed in their lives?

    She had to declare bankruptcy after getting into reckless credit card debt.

    He had an extramarital office affair that led to a messy and costly divorce.

22. How have they built their home life?

    The family eats every dinner at the kitchen table together.

    The family routinely takes adventurous vacations as a group.

23. What triggers appear to be part of their reactions?

    He gets aggressive when his accountant questions his decision-making.

    She nervously moves around when her stepmother comes to the home.

24. What type of image do they seem to project?

    He appears to be a tightly wound perfectionist.

    She conveys a Zen-like, easy persona.

25. How do they manifest the areas in their life that are important?

    She attends church every single Sunday regardless of where she is.

    He is part of a weekly golf league to network with business colleagues.

26. How do they typically dress?

    She always dresses to impress when she's with her friends.

    He wears sweatsuits anytime he isn't at the office.

27. How do they eat?

> They have embraced a vegan lifestyle.

> He grills steaks and potatoes every chance he gets.

28. What activities do they register for or volunteer at?

> The family serves meals at the local shelter.

> He is a member and attends weekly Rotary meetings.

29. What are their spending habits?

> He's skeptical of saving because he prefers to have fun with his money.

> She pays off her credit card every month without fail.

30. How are they raising their children?

> They send their children to a private Catholic school.

> He requires that the kids work for an allowance.

31. How were they raised?

> Her parents went through a bitter divorce when she was nine.

> His family held strict, conservative Baptist rules.

32. What are the cultural variables to consider?

> His parents were immigrants who spoke in their native language at home.

> She has lived her entire life in metropolitan cities.

33. What are the faith-based aspects of their lives?

> She is agnostic.

> He is a devout and practicing Muslim.

34. What was their upbringing?

>He was raised in a rural community with little access to trendy shops.

>She was brought up in extreme wealth and privilege.

35. How do they use technology?

>Her preference is to text when she is avoiding a difficult conversation.

>He screens and avoids phone calls when he is stressed at work.

36. What are their physical considerations?

>He has a heart condition that is accelerated during stress.

>She is extremely petite and fine-featured.

37. How are their living conditions?

>They try to reduce their carbon footprint by recycling.

>They live in a sprawling house filled with priceless art.

38. How is their hygiene?

>In public she always wears make-up and perfume.

>He doesn't shave or shower with regularity.

39. What types of transportation do they use?

>The family shares one vehicle and they use public transit.

>She drives a new Mercedes-Benz that is filled with all the best technology.

40. What other subtle messages are they providing?

>He chats idly anytime there's silence.

>She keeps a continual checklist to track her accomplishments.

This isn't an exhaustive list, but rather serves to generate curiosity about the information people present to the world. Conflict is often the result of both internally held values and their external presentation. When we bridge the two, we get a fuller understanding of the dynamics people exhibit. By delving into the detective work of determining who people are, we increase our likelihood of helping them chart their conflict management path. Using imagery, illustrations, and imagination ignites energy that can be used to create conversations about conflict that result in positive outcomes. In a sense, imagery gives people permission to bring their internal states to life in tangible ways so that they are better seen, heard, and understood.

Imagery Touchpoints:

1. How could you incorporate the forty questions listed above into your interactions with others? How do the nuanced aspects of human behaviors provide insightful information into the human condition, especially as it pertains to conflict?

2. How would you assess your skills of observation, detection, and attention to detail in various facets of your life? What areas could you improve upon? How would your conflict management practice be served by enhancing your holistic intuition skills?

3. What has it felt like when you believed someone understood your essence and connected with you in a way that was genuine and meaningful? How can you develop this into your ability to draw out people's imagery and illustrative representations about conflict?

Imagery Snapshot: *Using reflective, exploratory, and investigative questions can help develop understanding, empathy, and responsiveness to meet people where they are in their conflict journey through the mindful practice of helping identify markers that shed light on what conflict scripts they may internally hold.*

Liberty Training

If I asked you to imagine a horse, you might picture it with or without a saddle. The mental image may or may not depend on your experience or exposure to horses. I have ridden horses a handful of times, and I was always seated in a saddle. In fact, my first lesson focused on mounting and dismounting a horse wearing one. When I picture a horse, however, I think of the majestic animal without it. Despite my first-hand experience with horses, my imagery does not include any horse-riding equipment.

Last summer, I had the opportunity to take my kids to The Dancing Horses Theatre in Delavan, Wisconsin. These amazing animals perform to choreographed music with the partnership of their trainers. I purposefully use the word *partnership* because the horses aren't saddled. The horses and trainer quite literally weave throughout the stage without the horse traditionally tethered. I was fascinated by this, so the kids and I went on the tour afterwards. This is where I learned about liberty training.

Liberty training is the intentional decision to train the horse to perform while simultaneously giving it freedom.[39] This interplay works when the trainer recognizes the unique attributes of the horse and then tailors the interactions to suit its needs. The trainer is ultimately in charge, but the horse is recognized in the process. Horse and trainer coexist through mutual respect, understanding, and freedom.

The approach to liberty training is different from traditional horse training methods. For one, to begin liberty training, a trainer must first get close to the horse by studying it, talking to it, and experiencing it in environments outside of work or instruction. This approach counteracts other training methods. Carolyn Resnick, who coined the phrase "liberty training" forty years ago, provides the following insights:

> *The first thing you need to do is surrender the opinions of others and your own and leave your agenda at the door so that you can step into your natural talents, the ones you were born with, to train a horse from their instincts. By observing a horse in this way, you will find that your horse becomes alive to his true nature, and in that state of mind, he will be open to a feeling of trust and will naturally follow your leadership.*

What if we applied this idea to the creation of our conflict imagery? Instead of subscribing to conventional beliefs about conflict, what if we decided to take a mindful attitude instead? Viewing our background in a natural state where we study it, talk to it, and experience it outside the throes of stress allows us to create a reciprocal relationship between our past and the intended outcome. Liberty training can apply to our conflict approach. Our mind acts as the trainer, creating a mental environment where respect, understanding, and freedom can exist so that a well-trained, but unbridled, approach to conflict results.

Liberty training is about balance. It recognizes the roles involved and authentically honors them. The role of the horse and trainer are neither diminished nor judged. Let's do the same and stop being so critical of conflict or of the fact that everyone has a past that informs their present view of conflict. Incorporating a reflective practice around disputes and the ways we have developed our perspective will allow us to move more freely through conflict without being compelled to saddle it.

Saddles create a level of safety and control. Nothing is inherently wrong with the use of a saddle, but issues can arise if there is an overdependence on it. When a horse can only be ridden with a saddle, a barrier always exists between it and the rider. An artificial construct crops up in the relationship, though, understandably, this is sometimes a requirement. The fluidity of liberty training, however, allows the natural gifts of each to surface without the constant need for the saddle. Riding equipment does have its place in liberty training, but the primary goal is to augment a natural bond between horse and trainer.

If you are feeling stifled in the process of trying to identify your approach to conflict, consider whether you are being excessively saddled by a way of thinking, a person, or an environment. It can be helpful to ask yourself broad, exploratory questions to garner insights about what might be impeding your ability to connect with your core.

1. Do you feel compelled to conform to tradition? Is there an aspect of your upbringing that informs your perspective that you don't believe is who you are at your foundation? What previous messages were relayed to you about conflict that tether you now? What beliefs about your personality do you hold onto that don't bring you freedom?

2. What do you surround yourself with? Who are your friends? What clubs, organizations, or groups do you engage with? How do you spend recreational time? What do you read or watch? Are there environments or energies that work against your nature?

3. How do you find ways to process life? Do you have a confidant? Do you have a religious or philosophical system in place? Is there a therapist, doctor, or professional who helps you address life? Are there unhealthy choices or patterns you use to cope?

When we identify areas in our lives that saddle us, we gain clarity on how to address them. The goal isn't to unburden ourselves from the saddle entirely, but to recognize the positive role it can play in our lives. Challenges, obstacles, and suffering can serve our greater good when directed in a way that brings about eventual freedom. Like liberty training, this starts with a spirit of observation and incremental adjustment upon reflection. A trainer doesn't start with complicated tasks when first engaging a horse. We should not expect ourselves to fully understand our conflict imagery upon initial reflection, and neither should we demand perfection from ourselves when we try to embark upon a new approach to conflict.

Keeping the goal in mind helps us take small, reflective steps. A flexible, authentic, and realistic approach to conflict is the intended outcome. This can be achieved with thoughtful direction and the appropriate mindset that freedom is not the same as chaos. Conflict management, like horsemanship, requires boundaries that elicit a framework for liberty. Mindful boundaries allow movement within healthy parameters so that unhealthy tethering is avoided.

When we take a liberty-based mindset, we give ourselves permission to align with what we deem to be healthy for ourselves.

We can release ourselves from the saddles we depend on. In turn, our perspective of others will also become freer. We give ourselves permission to see others more compassionately. When we align to our internal truths, it is easier to give others the freedom to align to their internal truths. This positive cycle begets energy that creates environments where constructive conflict management becomes feasible.

As you consider what your liberty mindset will be regarding conflict, ask yourself open-ended questions that elicit curiosity. It is okay—in fact, it is encouraged—to create outrageous and absurd ideas as you brainstorm.

- If I was an animal, I would choose to be

  _____.

- If I was two years old, I would tell my younger self _____.

- If I could choose any activity or hobby to participate in forever, I would embark on _____.

- If I could travel anywhere to explore my personality, I would go to _____.

- If I could be related to or become best friends with anyone, that person would be _____.

- If I was given a blank check, I would spend it on _____.

- If I could start any career, I would become _____.

The point of this exercise isn't necessarily to find the answers themselves, though they can be very insightful. Instead, the purpose is to explore how and why you arrived at the answers. It's also beneficial to look at what's below the surface. For instance, if you decided that Italy is the country to which you would travel to explore your personality, ask yourself why you selected that location. During this brainstorming, determining *why* matters more than what. Maybe you travel to Italy because your favorite artist is Italian, and you want to explore your hidden creativity. Maybe you travel to Italy because your family roots originate in this part of Europe, and you want a deeper family connection. Maybe you travel to Italy because it's a country you've yet to visit, and you want to see how you learn about a new culture. Why are you drawn to your answers to the questions? They are revealing. This process can become a tool to determine what adds meaning to your life so you can start understanding your authentic nature. Using the lens of liberty training, we pay tribute to the unique attributes of people by not demanding that perspectives and mindsets be identical. As you go through this process, your imagery related to conflict becomes uniquely yours.

When I went through my divorce, some of my feelings and responses surprised me. It's interesting to discover your emotions can still surprise you. Mine prompted me to look at what was truly my foundation. I discovered that I cared too much about the thoughts and opinions of others. I allowed uninvited feedback from various sources to harm me. My self-perception started damaging the very essence of who I was. How does a mediator, boss, mom, friend, daughter, and partner serve in any of these roles if she is silencing her identity during a season of painful conflict?

Therapy helped reveal imagery that encouraged better coping skills: bullet-proof glass. Earlier in this book, I discussed the description "Seatbelt Kiley" used by a coworker to identify her perception of my personality. While it is a fantastic phrase, it's not mine. I needed to land on my concept if I was going to become a better conflict manager during the various aspects of divorce (which reach much farther than dissolving the relationship). Therapy showed me it would be healthy to come to terms with the fact that much of conflict, even apart from divorce, is outside my control. I started visualizing these parts of conflict as the bullets. Because I couldn't run away from many of these challenges, I needed to find a way to better protect myself. This is where the bullet-proof glass concept entered my mental framework. I might have to remain in certain situations where I must hear and see what is going on—which bullet-proof glass allows—but I don't have to be permanently wounded by any of life's weapons used against me. I still had children to raise, an organization to run, cases to mediate, and personal relationships to preserve. The bullet-proof glass framework allows me to more objectively absorb facts and information relevant to those tasks. I don't, however, have to be subjected to the destructive nature of metaphorical bullets, even those that are carefully aimed or intended for protection. For instance, I had well-meaning friends provide their opinions on decisions I made during the divorce, and some hurt me profoundly. At the time, it didn't even matter whether the comments were meant for my good or my harm as the words pained me to the point of personal handicap.

The same might be true for you. You may experience conflict and challenges that hurt you, despite the very best intentions of those involved. This can create internal turmoil as you wrestle with how you feel and what relationships you want to stay engaged in. Or you might be asked to help manage or mediate conflict that others are experiencing, and you might not fully align with or understand why the dispute triggers people the way it does. You may even fundamentally disagree with the crux of the argument. This can be complicated to navigate.

Back to liberty training, which works because of the authenticity involved. In the same way, the concept of bullet-proof glass works for me because it is genuine to my spirit and my needs. It is important that you find your own message when you deal with conflict. Otherwise, the odds of longstanding success are minimized. The mental imagery and conflict management approach you adopt doesn't need to make sense to everyone, even those who may be intimately involved in the conflict with you. Your *outward expression* of it is what will likely resonate in the world. And even if it doesn't resonate with others, you will find more peace knowing you are pursuing and demonstrating the most genuine version of yourself. The imagery of bullet-proof glass gives me stronger mediator skills and better interpersonal skills when I relate with my children, friends, colleagues, and partner.

At the start of this book, I shared insights from other mediators because it helped start a conversation on the various ways people articulate their inner framework about conflict. Now it's your turn to reflect on what you wish to express to the world. You will know when you accurately capture it because the vibrations it conveys to you will be in tune with your spirit.

Imagery Touchpoints:

1. Was it difficult to answer the three questions aimed at revealing the potential saddles in your life? Is your personal horse and trainer mindset in balance or does an area weigh too heavily in your life? How much should you adjust or adapt to ensure authenticity results?

2. How did you fill in the blanks to the brainstorming questions in this chapter? What other questions could you ask to create more insightful responses about yourself?

3. Upon initial reflection, what might be the expression of your conflict imagery? Mine was bullet-proof glass, while other examples have been peppered throughout this book. What are your thoughts on what you might want to convey?

Imagery Snapshot: *The freedom to express our unique imagery comes with the understanding that flexible movement can occur within the parameters of healthy, established boundaries. This is revealed in authentic expression that reflects an identity and core, resulting in stronger skills in managing personal and professional conflict.*

Create Your Mirror and Put a Bow on It

This book is called *Conflict Imagery: Developing a Reflective Framework*. The idea is that we can move through conflict in a variety of ways. We can behave like a wall, a doormat, a window, or any entryway. Or, we can act like a mirror. Only 8% of the light reflects on the surface of glass, whereas a mirror can reflect 95% of the light.[40] This is done through the process of coating the glass with something metallic on one side and a solid covering on the other side. Most of us look at a mirror and just pay attention to the reflective surface. However, the glass and back covering create a durable structure that resists tarnishing. The combination of these three elements results in a way to capture a reflection. Then, an opportunity exists to frame the mirror in a fashion that is in keeping with personal style. The mirror presented on this book cover has a decorative frame surrounding it, although I could have chosen a variety of different frames. I could have even decided not to frame the mirror at all. Framing the mirror, however, allows form and function to come together. It's conjoining science and art.

The mindset we take regarding conflict creates our foundation. My previous mentality toward conflict was a guarded, defensive approach. Fear of not being perceived as being perfect caused me to respond to conflict in an overly protective way. Aggression masked my heart. I still struggle with this, but I have developed more capacity for openness and vulnerability. There was a period in my life when I couldn't have written this book and been transparent and candid about my struggles. With growth, I now continually try to remind myself that conflict provides me opportunities that would not otherwise exist. These challenging situations can be gifts of light if I allow it. Seeing conflict in this way has required the formation of a reflective practice that is in keeping with my spirit. Imagery has become a cornerstone of my practice. Specifically, the ideas surrounding reflection. If conflict is a form of light then a mirror serves as one of the best ways to harness it. I don't want the light to just passively move through, like it would with plain glass. I want a solid mirror to reflect this light. I want the process of reflecting the light to be framed in a way that is in keeping with my style.

One of the best ways to create a reflective practice regarding conflict is to thoughtfully assess your background to determine what contributes to your conflict mindset, both positive and negative. Think about the gestalt of your lived experiences, as they all influence your lens on conflict. Then, associate metaphors, analogies, symbols, icons, and philosophies that convey your internal state. When we identify and name our internal state, it becomes more understandable to ourselves and to the world. With understanding comes a foundation for more constructive management. The same reason we create to-do lists in our personal lives and create job descriptions within our organizations is the very reason to express your internal conflict state through an established framework that augments who you are at your essence. The process of memorializing to-do lists and job descriptions helps draw out what is going on in the mind to an articulated state. This named articulation reduces confusion, creates understanding, establishes expectations, and develops actionable steps. We don't want to be mind-readers as we navigate through life, so the same application benefits our conflict management approach. Precise osmosis doesn't exist in the world of conflict. Why leave your conflict management to chance? Why expect people to mindread your intent? Why enter a situation of conflict without a developed approach that captures who you wish to be? Why deal with conflict without thinking through how we want to manifest our values and philosophies? How we deal with conflict can be a gift to ourselves and the world.

A gift can be given without wrapping it. A gift can also be wrapped without putting a bow on it. The content is still the same. However, wrapping a present and attaching a bow signals to the receiver that what's inside is something special. It indicates that you took the time and effort to display the gift in a meaningful way. The process of gift-giving is about both the giver and the receiver. Rarely is it that only the receiver is the beneficiary of positivity during the gift exchange. The giver gets something beneficial out of the experience as well, typically feelings of generosity, selflessness, or awareness that flow from the giving experience. The bow is the symbol that pays homage to the relationship between giver and receiver.

Think of the imagery and conflict script that you identify as the bow on the metaphoric gift. Whether or not people identify their conflict imagery and script consciously, it does reside within them. Manifesting it purposefully and articulately is like presenting it for the world to unwrap. It sends a signal to the receiver that there is something of note being delivered. And just like a gift, it's up to them to decide how to use the present. Hopefully reciprocity grows from there.

When we move away from the perspective that conflict is inherently bad or that we must control every variable involved, we communicate to ourselves and the world that conflict is simply a facet of life that can be a gift to create meaningful and necessary change. Our imagery and conflict script is our intentional and unique message to the world that we are paying attention to what resides within us so that whatever we identify can be a gift. It humanizes and personalizes our internal state of conflict to externally manifest a relational model for others to use if they so choose. Seatbelt Kiley and the lioness have something to offer, even during the complex aspects of conflict, and perhaps even more so.

All perspectives must start somewhere. An oak dining table doesn't end up in a home without a lot of steps, and that process starts with finding the right tree. Eventually, the wood gets winnowed down into the proper, functional shape. The final product comes to life with sandpaper and varnish. The sandpaper removes the unnecessary parts of the tree to create a smooth piece of wood. The final layers of varnish serve to highlight, beautify, and also protect the furniture piece. In essence, the process of unveiling conflict scripts and imagery is like building the kitchen table. Start broadly, then take the finer steps to create the desired outcome. Smooth the piece so that it stands the way you desire. Then proclaim what you have manifested, with confidence, while also protecting your truth. Just as a novice carpenter typically apprentices under a seasoned, skilled tradesman, the same goes for the conflict management imagery process. Modeling and demonstrating exemplary skills is how the iterative learning process unfolds.

Using an upside-down triangular, or funnel-like, approach to identifying your conflict script or image helps ensure that you begin with a wide lens. Then, these larger markers can serve as benchmarks for the finer parts of our personality that inform our approach to

WHETHER POSITIVE OR NEGATIVE, START BROADLY AND CONSIDER THE FOLLOWING:

What lived experiences have impacted me?
What core values do I hold?
What behaviors do I demonstrate on a regular basis?
What activities do I engage in?
What do I surround myself with?
What is part of my daily existence?

= Self-Identified Conflict Script or Image

conflict. Some people find it helpful to historically plot their lives by marking the people, events, and experiences that occurred from childhood to present. Consider also the literal and metaphoric aspects. The clarity this identification process provides can help define our conflict script or image. It then serves as a hallmark for our conflict management approach. If we start too narrowly, we run the risk of focusing on the obvious, overt, or negative aspects of conflict. It's easy to get caught in the trap of automatically being drawn to the familiar or comfortable. The broad, upside-down triangular approach helps ensure you don't miss facets along the way that could be useful information for you to digest. Macro *and* micro processing is important when it comes to conflict awareness. This not only helps us with our own self-discovery, but also lays the groundwork for us to better understand those around us. This understanding creates a vessel for compassion, awareness, responsiveness, empathy, accountability, and consideration. And that's how healthy foundations are created.

Strong footings are required for structures to effectively weather all the elements of life. Sun, wind, cold, rain, hail, snow, and heat are just part of the natural components of living. An architect doesn't just design a building with walls to keep people out, though this can be one objective. Rather, a skilled architect knows that structurally sound walls serve as holistic guideposts for addressing both the external and internal elements of the building. While sunshine is beautiful and necessary, in large doses, it can destroy whatever the rays touch. And while rain can be damaging in big quantities, in proper amounts, it serves the landscaping quite well. Your conflict script or imagery should be crafted as a healthy boundary guidepost.

The boundaries and pillars of our existence are healthiest when designed, constructed, and conveyed properly through the process of honoring our internal truth. Establishing a blueprint for a construction team is a respectful means of memorializing the building process by giving the team members something tangible to study and observe. Blueprints can be refined along the way to ensure the final product reaches the intended goal through the constructive input given by various individuals involved in the project. Your self-identified conflict management script or imagery is a blueprint, and it's more than just a metaphorical statement, symbol, or image. It's the tangible, literal storyboard from which work and progress grows. Further, conflict imagery development is about creating a focused framework that constructively links the past with the present to guide a more empowered future. Our capacity for managing conflict is truly limitless through the influence, artistry, and strength of our imagination.

Imagery Touchpoints:

1. How does thinking about conflict management as a bow on a gift change or impact your mindset? Is there another visual that better exemplifies your perceptions of conflict?

2. What feedback do the six exploratory questions provided in this chapter give you? What further exploration do you need to do to create more clarity on your self-identified conflict script or image?

3. Think about a past context or situation in which your conflict script or image would have been helpful. How might you use it going forward? What people or situations are you initially comfortable with to trust sharing this information? How will you grow your confidence by owning your conflict script or image?

Imagery Snapshot: *The way in which tangible information is externally presented demonstrates an innate measure regarding how we value that information. The external manifestation and presentation of our self-identified conflict script or imagery conveys to the world that it's being treated like a bow on a gift.*

Conclusion

This book was introduced by addressing the elephant in the room: A divorced mediator giving advice about conflict. Let's end this book by addressing another elephant in the room: I am still not a perfect practitioner of conflict mediation. Hardly. However, I would hope that those who know me would say that my approach has developed with time, experience, and effort. I am more grounded in the essence of who I am. I am less defensive, and I am more open. I am less aggressive, and I am more supportive. I will likely always be Seatbelt Kiley as well as the lioness, but this gal knows it stems from a heart filled with care and concern for the marginalized. It's also the very reason I need the concept of bullet-proof glass to cope. I rest easier in these truths. Conceptualization of conflict imagery pointed me to deeper meaning; to the anchor of my spirit. Your self-identified conflict script or image should do the same for you. The process is worth exploring because it reflects and binds us to a clearer story. It creates the footnotes for self-generated ideology. Instead of attaching conflict with fear, this perspective helps us to reframe our approach. Finding your unique script or image should breathe energy and purpose into your life, no matter your path. Let it help you sail with assurance.

Follow and connect with me at www.outsightin.org.

References

1. "The Memorial." Oklahoma City National Memorial Museum, https://memorialmuseum.com/experience/the-memorial. Accessed 20 May, 2021.

2. Eisenberg, Ronni. "Why Do We Love to Collect Things?" RE: Ronni Eisenberg, 10 Feb. 2020, https://blog.ronnieisenberg.com/2020/02/10/why-do-we-love-to-collect-things/#.YHW_oW5FzIU. Accessed 13 April, 2021.

3. Mark, Joshua. "Ancient Egyptian Burial." World History Encyclopedia, 19 Jan. 2013, https://www.worldhistory.org/Egyptian_Burial. Accessed 10 April, 2021.

4. "What is Historic Preservation?" National Park Service, https://www.nps.gov/subjects/historicpreservation/what-is-historic-preservation.htm. Accessed 13 April, 2021.

5. "The 4 Major Benefits of Historic Restoration and Preservation." Vintage Millwork Restoration, 24 August, 2020, https://vintagemillworkrestoration.com/blog/the-4-major-benefits-of-historic-restoration-and-preservation. Accessed 13 April, 2021.

6. Goldammer, Kurt Moritz Artur. "religious symbolism and iconography." Encyclopedia Britannica, 12 Nov. 2020, https://www.britannica.com/topic/religious-symbolism. Accessed 21 May, 2021.

7. "Wheelhouse." Collins Dictionary, https://www.collinsdictionary.com/us/dictionary/english/wheelhouse. Accessed 21 May, 2022.

8. Britannica, The Editors of Encyclopaedia. "Arab-Israeli wars." Encyclopedia Britannica, 5 Apr. 2022, https://www.britannica.com/event/Arab-Israeli-wars. Accessed 21 May, 2021.

9. Maroney, Terry A. "Emotional Regulation and Judicial Behavior." California Law Review, vol. 99, no. 6, 2011, pp. 1485–555. JSTOR, http://www.jstor.org/stable/41345439. Accessed 21 May, 2022.

10. "Conflict Famous Quotes and Sayings." Great Sayings, https://www.greatsayings.net/sayings-about-conflict. Accessed 13 April, 2021.

11. Shonk, Katie. "What is Conflict Resolution, and How Does It Work?" Program on Negotiation: Harvard Law School, 28 December, 2021, https://www.pon.harvard.edu/daily/conflict-resolution/what-is-conflict-resolution-and-how-does-it-work. Accessed 5 February, 2022.

12. Fleming, Kiley. "A Transcendental Phenomenological Study on How Experienced Mediators Elicit Enhanced Capacity from Parties During Unscripted Aspects of Mediation." Creighton University, 26 August, 2020, http://dspace.creighton.edu:8080/xmlui/bitstream/handle/10504/128251/Dissertation%20-%20Fleming%2C%20K%5B634%5D.pdf?sequence=3&isAllowed=y. Accessed 5 December, 2021.

13. "About CAMP." Coalition of Agricultural Mediation Programs, https://agriculturemediation.org/about-camp. Accessed 5 Dec., 2021.

14. "What personality traits do plumbers have?" Career Explorer, https://www.careerexplorer.com/careers/plumber/personality/#:~:text=Plumbers%20tend%20to%20be%20predominantly%20realistic%20individuals%2C%20which,like%20to%20spend%20time%20alone%20with%20their%20thoughts. Accessed 5 December, 2021.

15. "Wayne Gretzky Quotes." BrainyQuotes, https://www.brainyquote. com/quotes/wayne_gretzky_383282. Accessed 1 May, 2022.

16. "33 Different Styles of Fishing." Van Isle Marina, https://vanislemarina.com/33-different-styles-of-fishing. Accessed 5 Deccember, 2021.

17. Popova, Maria. "A Brief History of Children's Picture Books and the Art of Visual Storytelling." The Atlantic, 24 Feb. 2012, https://www. theatlantic.com/entertainment/archive/2012/02/a-brief-history-of-childrens-picture-books-and-the-art-of-visual-storytelling/253570. Accessed 13 April, 2021.

18. Passarella, Elizabeth. "Survey: Do You Need to See a Photo with a Recipe?" Kitchn, 4 Jun. 2019, https://www.thekitchn.com/survey-do-you-need-to-see-a-ph-80803. Accessed 13 April, 2021.

19. "Seven Reasons People Don't Read Instructions." LearningStream, 1 Nov. 2017, https://www.learningstream.com/2017/11/01/people-dont-read-instructions. Accessed 5 December, 2021.

20. DeSilver, Drew. "What to know about the Iowa caucuses." Pew Research Center, 31 Jan. 2020. https://www.pewresearch.org/fact-tank/2020/01/31/what-to-know-about-the-iowa-caucuses. Accessed 13 April, 2021.

21. Leigh, Steve. "Caucus: An Aid in Mediation." Mediate, Mar. 2018, https://www.mediate.com/articles/leighs2.cfm. Accessed 1 May, 2022.

22. Selva, Joaquin. "History of Mindfulness: From East to West and Religion to Science." Positive Psychology, 29 March 2022, https://positivepsychology.com/history-of-mindfulness. Accessed 21 May, 2022.

23. "DNA as Carrier of Genetic Information." Magazine Science, https://www.magazinescience.com/en/biology/dna-as-carrier-of-genetic-information. Accessed 21 May, 2022.

24. "Grow Mustard Seed in Your Garden." Epic Gardening, 17, Mar. 2022, https://www.epicgardening.com/grow-mustard-seed. Accessed 1 May, 2022.

25. "Salt." Phrases, https://www.phrases.com/psearch/salt. Accessed 13 April, 2021.

26. Jhangiani, Rajiv and Tarry, Hammond. "Principles of Social Psychology." EBook, 2014.

27. "Michelangelo." The Art Story, https://www.theartstory.org/artist/michelangelo. Accessed 21 May, 2022.

28. Harper, Heather. "The 23 Best Personality Tests In Ranking Order." WorkStyle, 7 Feb., 2022, https://www.workstyle.io/best-personality-test. Accessed 21 May, 2022.

29. "2021 State Agriculture Overview." USDA, 21 May, 2022, https://www.nass.usda.gov/Quick_Stats/Ag_Overview/state Overview.php?state=IOWA. Accessed 21 May, 2022.

30. Peterson, Cora, Sussell, Aaron, Li, Jia, Schumacher, Pamela, Yeoman, Kristin, Stone, Deborah. "Suicide Rates by Industry and Occupation – National Violent Death Reporting System, 32 States, 2016." Centers for Disease Control and Prevention Morbidity and Mortality Weekly Report, Vol. 69 No 9, 20 January, 2020.

31. Pedamkar, Priya. "Hardware vs. Software." Educba, https://www.educba.com/hardware-vs-software. Accessed 13 April, 2021.

32. Ehernberg, Ralph. "Route Mapping on the Lewis and Clark Expedition." Mapping on the Trail, http://edgate.com/lewisandclark/mapping_on_trail.html#:~:text=The%20primary%20maps%20prepared%20by%20Lewis%20and%20Clark,%20geographical%20latitude%20and%20longitude%20by%20celestial%20observation. Accessed 5 December, 2021.

33. "The Strongest Animals in the World: 15 of the World's Strongest Creatures." Safaris Africana, https://safarisafricana.com/strongest-animals-in-the-world. Accessed 13 April, 2021.

34. "Sydney Smith Quotes." Your Dictionary, https://quotes.yourdictionary.com/author/sydney-smith/599646. Accessed 21 May, 2022.

35. Berry, Nick. "A Square Peg in a Round Hole." Data Genetics, https://www.datagenetics.com/blog/september22012. Accessed 5 December, 2021.

36. Rau, Everett. "The Tree Nail in Timber Framing of the Past." DBPS, Dutch Tree Barn Preservation Society Newsletter, Vol 3, Issue 1, 1990, http://hmvarch.org/dbps-news2/dbpsnewssp90.html. Accessed 13 April, 2021.

37. "Jwaneng Mine." Debswana, http://www.debswana.com/Operations/Pages/Jwaneng-Mine.aspx. Accessed 5 December, 2021.

38. Cook, John. "God is in the Details." John D Cook Consulting, 30 Mar., 2008, https://www.johndcook.com/blog/2008/03/30/god-is-in-the-details. Accessed 5 December, 2021.

39. Resnick, Carolyn. "Liberty Training- What is it, and why does your horse need it?" The Resnick Method Liberty Horsemanship, 26, Oct., 2020, https://www.carolynresnick.com/blog/liberty-training-what-is-it-and-why-does-your-horse-need-it. Accessed 12 February, 2022.

40. Woodford, Chris. "Mirrors - The Science of Reflection." ExplainThat Stuff!, 21, Jun., 2021, https://www.explainthatstuff.com/howmirrorswork.html. Accessed 12 February, 2022.